The Big Muddy

- a canoe journey down the Mississippi -

by Sylvie Nickels

Illustrations by Tom Price

Oriole Press

Published by:
Oriole Press,
c/o Jane Geddes, 18 Summerfield, Oxford OX1 4RU

Typeset by:
Jane Geddes Publishing & Design,
18 Summerfield, Oxford OX1 4RU.

Printed by:
Antony Rowe Ltd.,
Bumper's Farm, Chippenham SN14 6QA.

ISBN 0 9518670 0 8

For George, of course

About the author

Sylvie Nickels has spent over 35 years as a travel writer
and editor. She has journeyed world wide though specialised
in the wilder or remoter areas of northern Scandinavia,
Yugoslavia and Eastern Europe. In addition to her travel
books she has published articles in many national
newspapers and magazines. At a time in life when most
people seek ease rather than exertion, Sylvie took up long
distance canoeing with her husband, lecturer and explorer
George Spenceley. When they are not tackling some new
venture, they live in a village in Oxfordshire.

About the book

This is the story of four months spent travelling the
Mississippi, most of it in an 18 ft open canoe. It was a
journey through the history and geography of North
America, with the unforeseen awaiting round every bend.
The participants in this story are many, but the heroine
and the villain are one and the same: the Mississippi in
her multiple guises.

The Big Muddy
- *a canoe journey down the Mississippi* -

Contents

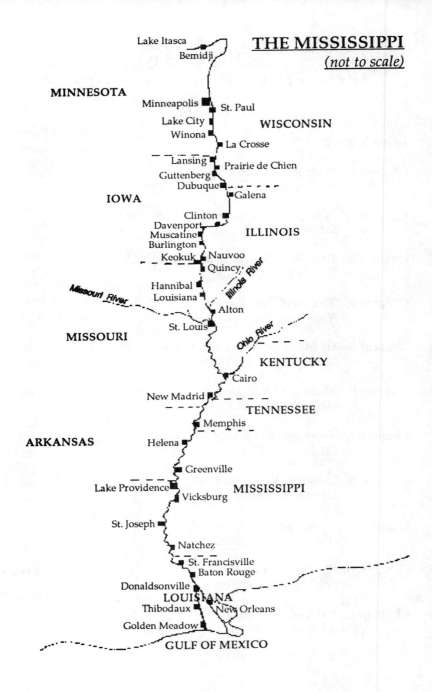

The Big Muddy

- *a canoe journey down the Mississippi* -

Introduction

"Be careful" American friends in Britain warned us when they heard of our intention to canoe down the Mississippi. "Ours is a violent country. Don't trust anyone." Most of these friends were from big cities; they probably knew as little about the heartlands of America as we did.

Why were we going to canoe it? A few years earlier, on the strength of some hours "training" on the Oxford Canal, I had allowed myself to be persuaded to canoe the full length of the Danube. Now, respectively in our mid sixties and fifties, we sought an even longer and bigger river. At least George did, for all his life he has thrived on challenges. I can, on the whole live without them! Yet I suspect that for me, too, there was a growing need to believe that middle age still leaves you with a lot of choices.

All the same I viewed the project with misgivings, mainly connected with my own physical and, even more, mental stamina. The amount of time, effort and financial investment needed for an escapade of this nature precludes any secret thoughts of opting out once it is under way.

As we read more about the river, it began to take on a massive personality of its own. As a main artery through the geography and history of a whole continent it obviously had a tremendous story to tell. But constantly repeated themes in every account written by our predecessors on the river, of whatever era, were of the unpredictability of its moods, the violence of its weather, and the loneliness of much of its shores.

How about going with someone else, I suggested to George on a number of occasions. But he would have none of it. So that was that.

Chapter One.
"You Guys take care"

From a grey lake on a grey day in north-west Minnesota a shallow stream scurried through a bridge of stepping stones and headed north-east. In silence I re-read the words carved on a wooden post beside it: "Here 1475 ft above the ocean the mighty Mississippi begins to flow on its winding way 2552 miles to the Gulf of Mexico."

Ardon joined me. "She's going the wrong way." I said. "And she's got longer. Our encyclopaedia said 2340 miles." The distance was engraved on my soul.

"She'll change direction in good time," Ardon said. "And your encyclopaedia is right; they've straightened out some of the curves."

Either way it seemed a crazy distance in a canoe.

George was busy trotting back and forth across the stepping stones, hands deep in pockets, with that hunched up look of suppressed excitement more appropriate to a truant schoolboy than a geographer in his mid-sixties. After 18 months of often frustrating planning I knew how he felt and, suddenly forgetting my own multitude of reservations, grinned at him. "Shall we go?"

Right at the beginning, when the whole mad idea was still just that, we were surprised to learn there were as many as 500 sinuous miles of the Mississippi before it even reached Minneapolis, the commercial head of navigation. As the idea evolved into a firm project George worked out a very approximate schedule for the four months we had available, making allowances for bad weather and, above all, for meeting people and seeing places. For us, after all, the canoe was a means to an end. The only record we were likely to break was to become the oldest couple to cover the greatest distance in the longest time. It became obvious, though, that something would have to be sacrificed. Determined to experience something of the wilderness country of the Mississippi's headwaters, we settled for a token 65-mile stretch from the source to Bemidji, then concentrating mind and muscle on the remaining 1800 or so from the Twin Cities of Minneapolis/St Paul to the Gulf.

Not many people had taken us seriously and even fewer were encouraging. The river passes through or borders ten States. The response from their respective tourist departments to our request for advice and information ranged from occasional cautious enthusiasm to frequent astonished disbelief. Even hard facts had been difficult to come by.

Our first major break came just a week before departure. Originally we had planned to buy a canoe in the States, hoping to sell it at the end of the journey. Now we received the generous offer of one on loan from the American Canoe Manufacturers' Union who had somehow got wind of our escapade. So, a few days earlier in that May of 1984 we had travelled out to the sprawling northern suburbs of Minneapolis and looked for the first time on the slender red vessel that we hoped would carry us down the 'Big Muddy': an 18 ft fibreglass We-no-nah. We tried her out there and then on a Mississippi in benign mood. Designed without a keel and devoid of any gear as ballast, she seemed to rock fearsomely. From the banks, We-no-nah's agent Betty Ketter watched impassively, firing occasional advice. A formidable lady, we could just picture her pounding West at the reins of a covered waggon.

"Do you think we'll make it?" George asked as we hauled the canoe out of the river.

"Guess you might," Betty said, but without conviction.

Next day we headed out of high-rise Minneapolis, our rented car crammed with gear and the upturned We-no-nah on the roof.

Our desire to sample the headwaters had posed some logistical problems, unexpectedly resolved by friendly contacts with Minnesota's Department of Natural Resources. Sure they'd be glad to help, they said, and so they did. Ardon Belcher, their Regional Trails and Waterways Coordinator, met us in Bemidji, arranging to come with us to the river's source so that he could drive our car back to be awaiting us at the end of our wilderness foray.

The discovery of the source of the Mississippi came rather late in the river's history - long after her broad waters much further south had carried countless thousands of explorers, traders, fortune-seekers, and no doubt a good many refugees from justice. A series of expeditions had resulted in various claims, and the precise source still exercises the minds of purists who care about such things. Most of us, however, have settled for Lake Itasca discovered by Henry Rowe Schoolcraft in 1832 with the help of Indian guides.

Initially I assumed Itasca was an Indian name, but it was not so. Perhaps with the idea of pre-empting all future arguments, Schoolcraft took the central syllables of *veritas caput* ("true head"), and so Itasca was born. Today it is protected within the boundaries of Lake Itasca State Park along with rare stands of red or white pine that escaped the axes of the 19th century logging operations. The park and its camping grounds are a popular destination among holidaymakers for whom one of the highlights is the bridge of stepping stones over which countless numbers can claim to have walked across the Mississippi.

There weren't too many of them, though, on that cool, damp day in late May. We put the canoe in a few hundred yards downstream from the stepping stones in order to avoid an awkward portage.

"See you back in Bemidji then," Ardon said. "Sure wish I was coming along."

We waved back at him until the first of the Mississippi's

million or so bends put him out of sight.

It rained, but only a little in the first hour and my initial preoccupation with the number of paddle strokes that separated us from the Gulf of Mexico soon gave way to more immediate matters, like adjustment to a whole new life style. The Weno-nah's behaviour, thankfully, was much less alarming now that she was fully and properly laden. The wilderness rewarded us almost immediately with the sight of an osprey riding the sky, and the embryonic Mississippi was positively skittish as she swerved jauntily in this direction and that across a wide expanse of marshes. There were also muscles to get back into training for neither of us had done any serious canoeing for a long time.

The DNR had provided us with very detailed maps of the headwaters, on which we marked the rather few rapids, the rather numerous sand banks liable to be exposed, as now, under low water conditions, and the changing terrain. Much of the latter consisted of flood plains of swamp and thicket of soggy and immeasurable acreage spreading to horizons rimmed by ridges of red and jack pine. Punctuating these expanses were areas of lowland or upland hardwood forests and conifer bog.

The forested sections we soon discovered meant steeper banks and a welcome briskness of current as the young river's meandering waters were funnelled through a narrow passage from one flood plain to the next. In high water our progress would certainly have been more impressive, and undoubtedly more fraught. As it was, our occasional bursts of speed alternated with a frequent need to get out and line the Weno-nah through rocky shallows.

But for the most part it was the flood plain that predominated. Across such expanses the junior river pursued an extravaganza of contortions that would have been wondrous to behold if it had not been so wearisome to follow. We spent much of our first full day negotiating a continuous succession of bends of 180 degrees and more, barely assisted by a laconic current. Often the narrowness of the river made it impossible to manoeuvre our 18-feet round such acute angles without backing up several times - a procedure made even more time-taking by rusty paddling techniques.

At quite frequent intervals the river divided, presenting us with a disconcerting choice of direction. Normally still water is a clear indication that a channel, however tempting, has no outlet. Poised at the dividing point we waited for the canoe to tell us which way to go, but she merely wavered indecisively. Finally we woke up to an infallible guideline for, proliferating on the river's muddy bed, the early long pale shoots of wild rice gently leaned in a current that was otherwise invisible. By late August, Ardon had told us, sections of the river would be almost choked by the mature plants and the harvesters would be out in force poling through the wild rice beds. But that was months ahead and, for the moment, they provided welcome signposts.

All the same for long periods the distant rim of forest on the horizon remained discouragingly remote. The immediate terrain consisted of tangled thickets of hazel and dogwood, or soggy marsh, from which a constant barrage of squeaks and warbles told of intense if invisible activity. From time to time a muskrat slid from bank to bank ahead of us or, briefly glimpsed, a painted turtle flopped from log to water.

"I'm beginning to understand," I said, "why Ardon was so discouraging about our idea of camping 'wild'. Seems the DNR have bagged the only clear dry spaces large enough to carry a few tents."

There were half a dozen of their camp sites marked on the map, with names like Coffee Pot and Bear Den. In the event, in most respects they qualified as 'wild' anyway, their amenities limited to a couple of primitive loos, a water pump or tap, and a few picnic tables and benches. Just then we were aiming for one called Stumphges Rapids. The name at least gave hope of speedier waters.

Rather soon we had our first encounter with an obstacle that the DNR could not mark on their map. Rounding yet another bend we found our way blocked by a shaggy construction of branches, twigs and mud that spanned the river from bank to bank. Nosing into it we surveyed the amazing structure with admiration.

There seemed only one practical way to tackle it. Cautious

reconnaissance showed that the beaver dam was quite solid enough to stand on and, in due course, with much heaving and shoving we managed to haul the canoe across with a minimum of unloading. After the first two or three our admiration of beaver dams began to wear thin and unpractised muscles to protest. It also became clearer why Ardon had suggested we allowed as much as four days to cover the 65 miles to Bemidji.

We were approaching our fourth dam when we heard the startling sound of human voices behind us. Four sturdy men in two aluminium canoes hove round a bend, paddles raised in greeting. In impressed silence we watched as, with furious application of their paddles, they hurled themselves at the beaver dam. With the canoe once balanced across it, the rear man edged forward and both occupants bounced up and down until the canoe and its load tipped down the other side.

"That is some technique" George said admiringly. Alas, not one to which we could subject our fibreglass We-no-nah even had she been ours to break up.

They grinned back at us. "How far you guys going?"

Obviously just then New Orleans seemed as unreal to George as it did to me, for he said, "Bemidji. But we're making for Stumphges Rapids tonight."

"We'll have a fire going. See you."

For quite a long time their heads were visible bobbing along above the rim of shrubs ahead of us as the river squirmed this way and that, until at last even their voices faded into the unquiet of the wilderness. Eight miles remained and they seemed interminable. But happily the beavers now gave us a respite, the flood plain changed to forest and faster waters added their encouragement.

Stumphges Rapids turned out to be not so much an official campsite as a tiny clearing among the trees, just big enough to accommodate a couple of tents and the fine camp fire that, true to their word, our dam-busting friends had well under way. The temperature had plummeted and it was a very welcome sight. As they helped us to haul the canoe up on the shore and unload, they introduced themselves: Bill, Blayne, Gerry and Smithy - a farmer, a teacher and two boat-builders who had briefly abandoned the family hearth for a taste of the wilderness. We thanked them for their help and, again, for leaving just the right space for our tent, and again for the coffee that was immediately proffered.

"Gee," said Smithy, "you don't have to be so darned polite."

"We're British, we can't help it," I said. "You'll just have to get used to it."

Smithy grinned and said he'd try. "He's a townie," Bill explained. "Guess he's not used to such fine ways."

It set the mood for that bitterly cold but warmly convivial evening. Fascinated they watched us make camp.

"That's a great tent," Blayne said, as we made the final adjustments to the flysheet of our compact Saunders' Hillsport and stowed away our considerable gear under the protective covering it provided by either entrance. "And that's quite some load you guys are carrying. Say, how about that aloo-minum box?"

The box, which could be padlocked to the canoe, was our most precious possession. One of the most constant and tedious problems of our Danube expedition a few years earlier had been protecting gear both from the elements and from the wash of passing vessels. We never really found a satisfactory solution, and our days were often bedevilled by time-taking and wearisome mopping-up and drying-out operations. For this escapade engineering friends in Cambridge had tailor-made this magnificent box for us in aluminium to fit amidships. In it, hopefully all our most valued possessions - photographic equipment, film stock, sleeping bags, medical supplies, best clothing - would be kept dry whatever the conditions. It was also earmarked as a wind shield for the stove, a table, a seat or a back rest as each need arose. Around it fitted the tent, food box, cooking gear, rucksacks and an incredible miscellany of odds and ends. A smaller waterproof bag at each end of the canoe protected our immediate needs during the day - binoculars, camera, notebooks. Yes, it was "quite some load."

On the lid of the box George had fixed lettering that read "Mississippi Paddle", so we now confessed our true intentions and were rewarded by genuine admiration and envy, without a hint of reservation. It made a refreshing change.

While we heated the contents of a couple of tins of stew and carrots over our Coleman stove, appetising aromas of grilling venison wafted over from the camp fire. It was taken for granted that we would share in it and, by the time we had done so and sampled an interesting assortment of strips of dried beef and fruit pieces, the popcorn was being roasted to go with the next round of coffee. Squatting round the fire we told them more about our plans, swapped views of current international crises, compared rates of taxation and inflation and the social ills of our respective societies.

"I just love the way you guys talk," Blayne said at one point. "Like those BBC nature programmes."

"Yeah," said Smithy, "You're even startin' to talk like 'em. But I guess those British programmes are OK. Remember that one about some palace that's gotten a zoo?"

"Woburn Abbey?"

"Yeah. Abbey, that's what it was. That guy who owns it - guess he's some kinda lord - the way he could handle them animals was really somethin'."

In a momentary silence I was suddenly aware of the darkness now deep beyond the firelight, and the way the sounds of the wilderness had stilled except for the nearby murmur of the Mississippi scuttling over rocks. Then a distant howl brought a response, followed by several more.

"Coyote" Blayne said in answer to my unspoken question. I got up stiffly, reluctant to leave the roasting heat. "Going to the loo," I said, and left George to explain this addition to our friends' growing Old World vocabulary.

As we lay huddled in our sleeping bags that night, the temperature plummeted to 22° F. From the neighbouring tent, quiet voices gradually petered into silence. "At a rough estimate," I whispered, "we've got only 2,285 miles to go." "And one day," George whispered back prophetically, "We'll be thinking back to this freezing night with enormous nostalgia."

We had to ease open the frozen zips of the flysheet next morning and both tents bore a thick coating of hoar frost. Gerry had already got the fire going and, emerging from the other tent, Blayne announced in clipped tones "I think I will go to the loo," grinning at me as he headed for the bushes.

Early shafts now slanted through the trees creating pools

of illusionary warmth in which we stood stamping numbed feet as we supped our cereals and coffee. On a tighter schedule than ours, our four companions broke camp rather more briskly amidst much banter. We waved them off from the shore, final gems of advice still reaching us as they rounded a bend in the river. "You guys take care," bawled Smithy. It was the last we heard as they finally disappeared.

We made rather a mess of the rapids which did indeed lie round the next curve. Though short they required some manoeuvring during which I failed to distinguish between draw and push strokes, and twice we got jammed on the rocks. After that things went better and for the next couple of days conditions were near idyllic. The sun shone, the current was noticeable and the river, now a little wider, far easier to negotiate. And the world breathed new life.

As our eyes and ears began to adapt to movement and sound, we became a little more adept at sighting some of the countless companions that shared the wilderness with us. From time to time there were glimpses of white-tailed deer beating a retreat across the marshes. Eastern kingbirds bickered in the thickets and kildeer spurted low over the water ahead of us, piping vigorously. A northern harrier quartered a swamp in search of a meal. Baltimore orioles glowed brilliant orange among a grove of jack-pines. Once an eerie scream drew our attention skywards as a loon hurtled over our heads.

Most often visible were the muskrat and the painted turtles. Of the beaver there were plenty of signs, not only in the form of dams and shaggily built lodges on the shore, but many a tree trunk bore evidence of their felling operations. It might take several days for a beaver to down a large tree, Ardon had told us; but give it a sapling and it would chew its way through in a couple of hours.

Just before our next camp in a grove of red pine at Bear Den we found a young man waiting expectantly on the shore. He had a pair of binoculars round his neck and his face lit up when he saw ours. "Some men said a couple of Britishers were coming through," he said in a soft Southern accent that originated from almost as far from this lonely northern place as did ours. "I'm Jerry Doggett."

16

He came over to the camp site later that evening and we talked of birds and conservation over a cup of tea. "My first cup of real English tea," he said as George poured boiling water over a tea bag bought in Minneapolis, and seemed so pleased that we hadn't the heart to disillusion him. He told us of a pair of nesting loons he'd found on a nearby lake, and then spoke of his deep concern for the ultimate fate of the Mississippi headwaters.

We had already noticed from the DNR maps that the buffer of wilderness separating river from farmland, especially along the last dozen miles before Bemidji, was disturbingly narrow. Its protection depended, we learned, on a complex inter-relationship between the county, State and private interests that owned those shores. At one stage Congress had intervened with the aim of making the survival of the remaining wilderness a Federal concern. But after years of inaction, negotiation and rival proposals, the river's fate was still unresolved. A Mississippi Headwaters Board, formed by a coalition of the local counties concerned, had come up with their own management plan. Jerry had great misgivings that such interests would show the kind of objectivity essential for the long term protection of the area. And we were inclined to share them.

At our last camp at Iron Bridge a disposable plate fixed to a picnic table bore a scrawled message: "George and Sylvie - to those crazy guys from across the Big Water, be careful on your trip. Let's hear from you - your dam-busting friends, Smithy, Bill, Gerry and Blayne."

It was a perfect camp looking out over immense marshes that glowed gold in the northern evening light, and we stayed up until the intense cold drove us into our sleeping bags. With 50 or so miles behind us, and mind and muscle now adapting to the nomadic life, all seemed very well with the world.

Ironically it was next day in the final miles to Bemidji that I got my first real attack of jitters. The day began auspiciously enough with magnificent conditions: a good current and an early morning mist coiling off the water in the strengthening heat of the sun. The Iron Bridge itself spanned the river just round the corner from the camp site. As we slid beneath it, cliff swallows rose swerving and dipping in swarms from a veritable ornithological crêche in its structure. We paused a moment to ride the current and look back at the row upon row of nests, each with its fluffy pack of chicks crowding the entrance.

"Shades of Jerry Doggett," George said soon after, as we slid past the first houses of our journey - modern summer houses by the look of them, underlining our Southern friend's fears for the river's future. For the moment there were not too many of them, and fairly soon alternating marsh and farmland became alternating marsh and woodland once more.

It was as we passed from one of these to the other that a huge shape rose from the left bank and for a few rare and precious seconds we stared in wonder at the white head and tail and majestic wing span of a bald eagle, only feet above our heads. As startled as we were the magnificent creature lost hold of its dinner, and from its talons its slippery silver victim dropped into the river, just missing our bows. It was a view in a lifetime.

Ardon had warned us of some sections where the river ran through virgin lowland hardwood forest. "It can be kinda tricky," he'd said, and very shortly we discoverd why. Despite lowish water the current really was now quite brisk and this factor alone would have been welcome. But totally unexploited the forest was left to pursue its natural cycle undisturbed. In various stages of life and death, ash and basswood, maple and aspen, leaned or lay across the fast-moving water providing an obstacle course that fully tested George's skill as steersman in the stern and my nerves as crew in the bows. Memories of an earlier frightening adventure that I had fairly successfully stifled during our planning of the expedition now surfaced in a rapid succession of mental images that no attempts at logic would displace.

We had been canoeing the upper reaches of the Dordogne in France. Up to then our joint ventures had been almost entirely on waterways of some stature, most notably the Danube. But the young Dordogne below Argentat was still a frisky mountain river, punctuated by Grade One or Two rapids that, after initial care, we began to tackle with unforgivable lack of caution.

It was on the third afternoon that we met our Waterloo. From a stony islet we had paused to choose our route. On one side the water was too shallow; on the other a deep swift channel, half blocked by an uprooted tree, surged beneath overhanging branches which would need to be avoided at all costs. It looked simple, but we mis-read the river and planned tactics that were disastrously wrong. Caught up in the current the canoe swirled round like a top and hit the fallen tree side-on. The next moment we were floundering in the water, borne helplessly along like so much flotsam. So were our cameras, camping equipment, sleeping bags, rucksacks, food box and a myriad items, above all the life jackets we should have been wearing all caught up in a headlong rush towards the distant Bay of Biscay.

We clung to the upturned canoe, one at each end. "We must keep calm," I remember saying, my whole being swamped as much with fear as with water.

In the nightmare sequence of events that followed I grabbed futilely at objects that drifted within reach: the tent, a paddle, one shoe. George struggled desperately to free an ankle entangled in one of the painters and pinned under the canoe. For seconds that seemed eternal the canoe slid out of my grip and I thrashed about frantically until I saw the bow painter carried towards me by the current and pulled myself back. Deep, fast and implacable the Dordogne surged on. A minor rapid came and went bringing new fears of what could well lie round the next corner. All thought of salvaging any possessions was abandoned, and still we hurtled on.

At last, after about three kilometres and an emotional eternity, the Dordogne summarily spewed us into a backwater where, in almost stagnant water, the canoe and us with it rotated slowly 50 yards or so from shore. George finally freed his foot and eventually we struggled to land through a thick soup of flotsam on an overgrown bank.

For a long time after the event I could not stop my thoughts from entering the imaginary realm of might-have beens. Always the water was black, always George was being pulled beneath it, and always there was the stark choice. Would I? Could I? And now they flooded back, those might-have-beens from the Dordogne past superimposed on the Mississippi present.

I chose the wrong moment to voice my thoughts. "For heaven's sake," George said, exasaperated, as one of our manoeuvres failed and we flailed our way through a tangle of rotting trunks and vicious brittle branches. "It's nothing like the same situation. You couldn't drown in this if you tried."

Could you not indeed, I thought, if you got pinned under by the current, or rendered senseless by any of countless obtruding objects, or your foot got caught up in the painter...? But I shut up.

At times it was impossible to see a way through, with fallen trees from both banks all but blocking the river; but with enforced practice and despite me George became very adept at the "ferry glide", a technique by which you position the canoe and allow the current to carry it sideways across the river. In the occasional restful interludes even I could register the considerable beauty of this untamed waterway as the sun filtered through the canopy of leaves dappling the dancing water; but much of the time it was the primeval eeriness and aura of death that dominated my own dark thoughts as we slid over layers of rotting trunks entwined with weed between sentinels of dying trees. Walt Disney could have made much of it.

The relief when the river finally emerged into a landscape of open sunlit meadows was enormous. Ahead lay little Lake Irving connected by a narrow channel to Bemidji's lake. Within a couple of hours I was heading for a telephone, thoughts of the Dordogne past and the Mississippi future firmly supplanted by the joyous prospect of a few days of respite.

Chapter Two.
"There's a tornado down the road"

After our interlude on the headwaters it felt strange to be back in the big-city, high-rise world of Minneapolis. Canoeing is a way of life in Minnesota but not, it seemed, on the Mississippi. Did we realise, the Minnesota Department of Tourism had written some months earlier, that below the Twin Cities it was "a vicious unpredictable body of water... and cross currents and swirling water, pleasure boats and barge traffic made for a very difficult voyage?"

Happily, the ever-to-be-blessed Department of Natural Resources continued with their encouragement and promised to put us in wherever we chose on a river that now fully merited its many epithets and, not least, the "Big Muddy". In order to catch up on a slightly retarded schedule, we decided to launch ourselves half way down Lake Pepin, about 60 miles south of Minneapolis.

Thankfully George returned our rented car which he had always regarded as a slightly immoral adjunct to the expedition, and on a Sunday morning Steve Thorne and his son collected us from the Holiday Inn. By the time we had side-tracked for some sightseeing on the way it was late afternoon when Steve helped us launch our We-no-nah from a pebbly shore.

Suddenly the moment had come and there was no decent way of backing out.

"Good luck. Wish I was coming with you," said Steve, who was one of the few who didn't think we were either heroic or demented. He gave us a final shove and we slid off across glass-smooth water into a golden evening. "New Orleans, here we come," I announced silently to the sky, and felt for once almost optimistic.

Lake Pepin is not really a lake but a broadening of the river, some 20 miles long, up to 4 miles wide between the beautiful wooded bluffs of Minnesota and Wisconsin. It is also famous for two things. One is water ski-ing, invented by a citizen of Lake City on its shores in the 1920s, and the other is the frequent violence of its waters. The prevailing winds in the Mississippi valley we already knew were south-easterlies. It was only next morning after a restful first camp near Lake City that we learned with what speed and effect they can turn a placid expanse of water into oceanic turbulence.

Within a few minutes a smooth glide had become a hideous bucking and plunging between furrows of surging white-topped ridges. It took an hour to crawl across a bay and creep thankfully into the shelter of Lake City Marina where our first day's paddling ended ignominiously at around 10 a.m. after a total of two miles. But we had learned valuable first lessons concerning the unpredictability of the Mississippi and the river worthiness of our sturdy vessel.

With a new understanding of America's preoccupation with its weather, we bought a small radio in Lake City. The harbourmaster wasn't very keen for us to leave next morning either.

"She's going to blow at 15-30 mph; may be thunderstorms later," he said after calling the weather station. "Keep close to the shore and get her out at the first sign of trouble. This lake can be real mean." Then he grinned, looking round at the surrounding fleets of motor-cruisers. "But it's folk like you that make my job interesting."

Hunched in the bows I reflected gloomily on the injustices of feeling scared even while our first main river camp was still in sight. There was some comfort in the proximity of the Burlington Northern Railway and the road from which a truck would occasionally honk a greeting. But the banks were steep and rocky, and getting out would have presented problems almost at any point.

In the event it wasn't necessary. Progress was slow, but imperceptibly the distant southern narrowing of Lake Pepin at its junction with the Chippewa river began to seem less remote. By late afternoon we were in the first of the sloughs - pronounced *sloos* - those narrow arms of the river that were to be so much part of our lives in the weeks ahead.

We camped that night on our first sand bar and the tent blew down in the middle of the night, confirming that one of our first purchases must be some special sand pegs. Yet it was a lovely spot, our first taste of the wilderness which we had not expected to be such a predominant feature of our journey on the main river, despite Steve's brief geography lesson over our last dinner in Minneapolis.

We had just acquired the Upper Mississippi River Navigation Charts revised annually by the US Corps of Engineers. There were an amazing 150 large sheets of them covering the first 868 navigable miles from just above the Twin Cities to Cairo, where the Ohio river came in. At 2-inches to the mile they showed in incredible detail every headland, islet, bay, channel, navigation aid and hazard. As we turned the pages and got the visual impact of the river's staggering complexities, alternately weaving through a fragmented landscape of forest, marshes and sand bars, then opening into gigantic lake-like pools, I began fully to appreciate the size of our undertaking for the first time. Even the calamitous descriptions written by our predecessors on the river (none of them in canoes) had been tempered by the unreality of distance.

There are 29 locks and dams punctuating the 670 miles between the Twin Cities and St Louis, and the river pattern they created was pretty consistent. Above the dams lay the great pools, up to 3 unbroken miles wide; below them the river divided into a labyrinthine system of sloughs between the islands and sand banks. At varying distances from either shore rose steep wooded bluffs, sometimes with space for a riverside community but more often not.

"You won't find the locks any problem," Steve said. "But

sometimes you may find it better to portage over into the sloughs away from the navigation channel. You'll be out of the way of the traffic, and you'll see more wildlife."

Navigation aids and hazards were marked in red. There seemed an alarming number of the latter but on closer examination most of them were submerged features like wing dams or bank protection: nothing, Steve assured us, for a canoe to worry about. Nor, he said, need we concern ourselves more than by the exercise of a little caution with the stump fields that filled considerable expanses of the sloughs and pools. We'd already read about them. They were literally the stumps of the forests felled when the lock-and-dam system was created.

"When the water's high you won't even know they're there. When it's low, you'll see them just below the surface of the water. They're bad news, of course, to anyone with an engine. When you're travelling the sloughs, you'll know what it used to be like all the way. Those islands are what's left of the bottomlands hardwoods. Most of them are protected - part of the Refuge that stretches pretty well all the way from Lake Pepin way down to Rock Island."

We had a leaflet about it. The Upper Mississippi River National Wildlife and Fish Refuge, as it was officially designated, is a gigantic nature reserve of some 195,000 acres of wooded islands, marshes, sloughs and backwaters along the State borders of Minnesota, Wisconsin, Iowa and Illinois.

"But it's not quite what you think of as a nature reserve. Sure it's protected land, but it's protected for the hunter as well as the hunted, like most of the areas controlled by so-called conservation societies here. You know 100,000 deer get shot by a quarter of a million hunters in Minnesota alone? - and that's not counting the bow-and-arrow brigade. That's in a season lasting a maximum of 10 days. Some of 'em only bring their guns out once a year; sometimes they shoot each other by mistake! It's a dangerous time to be out and about. Still, our gun laws are better than in most States and I guess we've still got a lot of game."

For several days after the night our tent blew down, the wind raged relentlessly. After breakfast in the little town of Wabasha, we scuttled across the choppy main channel into the marginally calmer Indian Slough and so through a maze of channels into wide, shallow waters punctuated by sand banks and islets of grass and scrub through which our efforts to find a way were frequently brought to a halt as we touched bottom. It took ages and much wading to get through, and when we did it was to meet the full force of wind and waves battering our starboard side as we bucketed across more open water to the Wisconsin shore.

The navigation maps, supremely accurate in all that concerned the navigation channel, proved less so for the lesser sloughs. In any case the topography changed according to the level of the river which was then somewhat high - and was to become much higher - so that larger islands had shrunk in size and smaller ones disappeared altogether. As far as I was concerned it was a day dominated by fear in which buried memories of our Dordogne escapade again surfaced starkly. The next day wasn't much better as we crept down the Wisconsin shore towards our first lock and dam, No. 4, at Alma. Here things brightened up considerably. There was no sign of commercial traffic and my worst premonitions gave way to grateful surprise as the majestic machinery of the lock slid into action, the gates slowly opened, a red light turned to green, and we paddled into the huge lock chamber feeling, and no doubt looking, very small. The lockmaster lowered a rope for us to hang on to. "Where you guys headed?" he asked, and shook his head either in wonder or pity when we told him. But he scrawled a sketch map for us, marking a short cut for canoes that saved us several miles to our next camp site.

We had learned about Great River Harbor back in Lake City. We reached it early that afternoon, our three days paddling having achieved a miserable total of 25 river miles, excluding deviations. For the moment the implications of this were lost in the joyful prospect of a patch of firm meadow under our ground-sheet, the availability of showers and a nearby restaurant as an alternative to camp cooking.

Apart from the restaurant Great River Harbor consisted of a handful of summer cottages and the offices of the marina whose small fleet of houseboats shuffled restlessly on their moorings in the gusting wind. Steve Wick, the energetic young president of this enterprise, came over while we battled to secure our flapping flysheet over the tent. I asked "Is your weather always so God-awful?"

He shook his head thoughtfully. "This sure is a mean streak. You heard the weather station? There's a front hardly moving, stretches from down in Louisiana to the Atlantic, right up the Big Muddy - floods in the Twin Cities, the Missouri over her banks, mud flowing through the streets in some places, cars floating away in others, and tornado touch-downs every which-way."

My mind froze. Don't be silly, I thought; tornadoes are things that happen to other people.

"You don't have 'em in England?" Steve looked surprised. "Yeah, well you'll recognise 'em, no problem. Look out for a sorta funnel-shaped cloud swirling down. It builds up terrific pressure and where it touches down, everything in its path just blows. I heard of a guy lifted clear out of bed, found himself in his barn, only the barn wasn't there any more and no more was the house."

"But can you see which way it's going?"

Steve grinned at me. "That's your tidy British mind! They can move any way or jump about or swing around or just get sucked back up into the sky."

George made a firm attempt to inject moderation into my wild imaginings. "Yes, but the track of a tornado's very narrow. It's a million to one it'll touch down just where you are."

"It can be a few yards or a few hundred wide." Suddenly Steve got the message. "But you're right - it's probably more dangerous trying to cross the highway."

With everything battened down, we strolled up to the main road and the Great River Inn. A Rolls Royce was parked outside, an Illinois number plate fixed over the original British one. The waitress was delighted with out accents.

"Do you like our car?" George asked, nodding at the Rolls through the window, but the real owner was at the table just behind him. In the convivial couple of hours that followed I forgot about tornadoes, and even the torrential rain that began half way through our meal seemed a mere inconvenience.

The manager of the restaurant insisted on driving us back to our tent. George was hastily securing and adding more tent pegs when the night was rent by a reverberating crash that sent even him diving, rather wide-eyed, into the tent.

"God that was close," he said in the infinitesmal moment before the next crash. Then the lightning began like an unsynchronised battery of faltering million-watt bulbs, the rain intensified into cataracts, and the wind became a raging beast beating at the flimsy walls of the tent.

I am not normally afraid of storms, but for the next several hours the uproar was horrendous. At some point a voice reached us out of the holocaust. "You folks OK in there? We've plenty of room at the restaurant and we'd be glad to have you."

"You go," George said, but even terror wouldn't allow me to face the awful shame of such a prospect. And if our gear were wrecked it would mean the early death of the expedition.

"There's a tornado warning 20 miles down the road," the voice bellowed.

"We're OK - thanks. It's very kind of you, but we'll stay," George yelled back.

Within our tiny cocoon of calm I alternately clung to George or to the nearest tent pole when it seemed it must collapse under the onslaught. I tried to think rationally but found rational thought impossible to pursue through my battered senses. I tried to pray, but even belief was reduced to meaningless gibberings. Nothing existed except mind-swamping noise and flashing lights and fear.

The core of the storm rolled on, returned and rolled on again, how many times I don't know for at last we slept fitfully. We awoke to a wind that was strong and steady, but to sunshine and a world that incredibly still appeared to be in one piece. The restaurant people came over once more to see if we were all right. Steve materialised from his home some miles away. Three of his houseboats, ripped from their moorings, had drifted several hundred yards down the slough, fortunately to be halted by overhanging bushes. We spent the morning helping him to retrieve them and putting our own shambles in order.

"That's quite a tent you've got," Steve said when at last there was time to talk. "That wind was gusting at 80 mph. A

27

tornado touched down about 50 miles away and several people died. There may be more to come. Hope it's OK, but I've booked you into a comp. room in Wabasha."

I could have hugged him, and did when we found that not only did "comp." mean complimentary, but the offer came from Anderson House, a restored building of great character and, in Midwest terms, some antiquity. It had been run as a hotel since its opening in 1856 and by the same family for four generations. In Ida's Old-fashioned Ice Cream Parlor we peered at framed covers from ancient issues of McCalls and Ladies' Home Journal. George reported classical nudes on the lavatory seats of the gent's loo and, in the absence of the live equivalent, it was possible to borrow one of the hotel's six cats for the night if you felt lonely.

Steve offered to drive us and our gear to Winona where we planned a 3-night stop only 22 river miles away, but I guessed George wouldn't accept and he didn't. In the event we covered the distance in a day and a half with only one major deluge. A delightful stretch through narrow winding sloughs, overhung by the willows and cottonwoods so predominant in these bottomlands, gave us a taste of how idyllic this journey could be. But the exposed roots of innumerable fallen trees were a reminder, too, of the violence that could penetrate even these sheltered ways.

By dint of portaging over a couple of dykes, we avoided both Locks 5 and 5A, but more importantly continued to benefit from the relative shelter of sloughs for much of the way. There were nevertheless some fearsome stretches of exposure to unremitting wind, not least on our final approach to Winona. This necessitated an alarming crossing of the navigation channel, side-on to a wind of some 25 mph that had perversely swung to our rear and, combined with an unusually fast current, it required the greatest efforts not to be carried past the entrance to our goal, Dick's Marina. From the marina's office, Greta came to help us unload our gear. She told us she had survived the war destruction of Dresden and quite obviously intended no irony with her first greeting "It's good to hear a British accent." We encountered this nostalgia for things European time and again.

Winona, with a population of over 20,000, seemed a major metropolis after the little riverside communities we had so far called on. In the heart of its main shopping precinct a fountain played beneath a statue of the Indian princess after whom the town was named, and who had flung herself to a dramatic death from a rocky prominence because she was denied marriage to the man of her choice. Our canoe also bore the name of this sad lady for the good reason that Winona was the home of We-no-nah Canoe Inc. As soon as possible we sought its young founder, Mike Cichanowski, to whom we were indebted for the loan of our admirable vessel. His single-minded dedication to canoes and canoeing - he is a top racing canoeist - became very apparent as we toured the works pausing, in an atmosphere pungent with fibreglass, to examine some of his many different hand-built models in various stages of completion. Mike was a prime example of go-getting American enterprise.

"I started building canoes back in high school," he told us. "Every time I thought I got it right I could see there was still some way of doing it better, and so I went on. And so it still is."

With a long list of awards to his credit he had obviously got it right quite a few times.

With our canoe and gear safely stowed at Dick's Marina, we revelled in the comforts of The Hotel, another restored golden oldie of the Midwest, this time from the 1890s. Sterling and Vi, schoolteaching friends from the Minnesota interior, collected us to drive up to Garvin Heights where we got our first bird's eye view of the Mississippi. For a moment we were silenced by the sight of our navigation charts transformed into life size; a vastness of water lacing the wooded Bottoms for several miles between the shore line bluffs of Minnesota and Wisconsin. Now it was possible to see the canyon-like course, albeit wide and relatively shallow, that the river had gouged out between the bluffs. Inland from these, and invisible from the river, the cornfields of the Midwest stretched immeasurable to the eye at an altitude of up to several hundred feet higher than the river itself.

Below us sprawled the town, spawned by the river and its

traffic back in the 1850s. As a reminder of those days a replica of the *Julius C Wilkie*, a turn-of-the-century stern-wheeler destroyed by a fire a few years earlier, has been sunk in concrete and dominated the riverside of Winona's levee park area. It housed a steamboat centre. The attendant left her post to join us in front of a photographic display.

"They used to float the lumber down from the Chippewa river to the mills here. We had some of the best-equipped sawmills in the country in those days." On the photographs the rafts of timber looked enormous, dwarfing the push-boat that nudged it along from behind; by the front of the raft a bow-boat apparently steamed back and forth, sideways to the current, to keep the whole thing on a straight course. "Most of the big houses in town were built by the lumber barons. Then they ran out of forest, and now the big houses are mostly turned into apart-ments."

Ironically the *Julius C Wilkie* looked down on the railway lines that eventually spelt death for the steamboat era and for many a riverside town. By 1920 steamboats were few and far between and the shallow-draft tows couldn't compete with the railroad that sprawled in all directions. Then came the Roosevelt response to the nation's economic ills. As part of his farseeing New Deal, Congress authorised a 9-ft navigation channel for bigger and more modern tows, and the system of locks and dams all the way from the Twin Cities to St Louis. The railways weren't happy but at least some of the riverside towns came back to life. Winona adapted better than many by diversifying into a range of small industries on the outskirts of town; but the population figures hadn't changed much in 50 years.

"And we haven't finished paying for the New Deal yet," many Americans told us as the story was repeated all the way down the river. But the Mississippi was back in business and the dollar didn't seem to be suffering too badly.

We passed some of the lumber barons' homes with their colonnaded porticos and elaborate gables one evening after a delightful supper with friends. It was still early so we wandered through the quiet evening streets towards the river, trying to visualise the bustle of the lumbering days behind the cracking plaster and peeling paint of old warehouses. Night hawks swooped for their supper in the dying light, and a restaurant was still open.

"Just a beer and a coffee please," I said to the young waitress. To our astonishment she went into paroxysms of mirth.

"Those accents," she gasped. "Oh, I just *love* those accents."

"I'm glad you like them," said George at which her hilarity only became greater.

She calmed down at last, brought our beer and coffee, and sat down to interrogate us about England, quelling her giggles as best she could.

Before leaving Winona we called on the office of the Upper Mississippi Wildlife and Fish Refuge.

"I sure wish I was coming with you," said Glen Sherwood as we explained our mission. He gave us the names of Refuge managers further downstream. "They'll be able to tell you where there are bald eagles' nests. There are some fine heronries off in the sloughs as you go down, too." We asked about the problems of conservation.

"Ours are special here because navigation has priority over conservation. You've probably seen some of the dredging operations?" We had. Dredgers virtually "vacuumed" the silt from the river bed, then blasted it through a cordon of mammoth pipes to spew it out several hundred yards away, creating huge sandhills or new sandbanks. "Well, the dredging and the constant shifting of silt because of tow turbulence is changing - has changed - the ecology of big areas. And that's not even to mention the big pools that came after the building of the dams in the thirties.

"Of course, the channel has to be kept clear and the water moving as the Corps wants it, but *where* they put all that dirt is something else. Still things are improving - slowly. Instead of dumping it in the nearest place it's now going where we want it - at least sometimes. But there's a long way to go." He grinned. "Talk to the Corps engineers and you'll probably hear another story."

We spent a convivial last evening with Mike Cichanowski and some of his canoeing friends, watching home-made videos of canoe exploits as we tucked into barbecued chicken and a variety of salads as only the Americans can make them. Mike and his brother Jerry decided to paddle with us on the first part of our next 28-mile leg to La Crosse. In answer to our query they said it would take us about eight hours.

"We mean at our speed not yours."

Mike grinned. "That is your speed. We'd do it in two!"

We put on our best performance next morning as we crossed the river and followed the Wisconsin shore in the lee of islands. Mike watched us appraisingly. "Paddle in rhythm together; you won't bob around so much. Don't bring your paddle so far back Sylvie - it's wasted effort. You've got to avoid anything that doesn't contribute to moving you forwards. Remember you've got a few miles of the Big Muddy to go!"

We wanted, indeed needed, any expert advice we could get. Mike put us through our paces with sweep strokes, bow strokes, cross bow strokes, and then said suddenly. "You're doing OK. We've covered 5 miles in half the time I reckoned it'd take you. Remember when you hit a boil, don't look at the water, but ahead to the horizon; then you won't feel giddy. We'll go back now, Jerry. Send us a postcard from New Orleans." And within minutes, even against the current, they were fast vanishing specks heading for a gap between the islands.

Our encounters with some of the 300 million tons of cargo that travel the river annually had so far been minimal - largely because we had mostly kept to quieter waters. We had, however, had the satisfaction of one or two close encounters with tows on the move and found that our We-no-nah rode the widely spaced swell of their bow waves with comforting confidence. At Lock 6 our fortunes changed and we coincided with two large tows waiting to go through.

Knowing it would take nearly two hours for each to complete the necessary double-lockage we moored by a floating jetty nearly a mile from the lock and champed at the delay. To our dismay just as the end of our wait appeared nigh a third and then fourth tow bore down on us. Once they had taken their place in the queue George was all for paddling past them to try our luck. As afternoon lengthened into evening I reluctantly agreed, praying they would not get under way in the meantime for the turbulence churned up by their screws was dramatic to see. We had never been so close to a tow before and the barges towered above us like mini cliffs as we hastened along their quarter-mile length. Thankfully we found another mooring close to the lock, just across the railroad lines of the Burlington Northern from the little town of Trempeleau. Two school girls came to inspect us. The chatty one introduced herself as Sharon.

"It's great the way you guys talk," she pronounced admiringly. "I sure wish I could go with you - never been to New Orleans. I guess you'll have a lot of adventures. Maybe you could write to me? I'm going to be an archaeologist when I leave school. Hey, I don't reckon you have to wait for all those tows and stuff to finish before you go through. My Pa works on the locks. Let's go ask."

Happily Pa agreed. "You get here first, you go through first," he said. "I'll tell the next captain to hold back."

With some relief we found ourselves at last the lonely occupants of the lock chamber. Pa leaned over the side. "You want a camp site? There's some great sandhills on an island about a mile on, port side."

That was the night we first saw the lightning bugs in their myriads, flickering their tiny batteries amongst the trees, as though a starlit sky had briefly become earthbound. A mist was snaking off the river and several tows throbbed past, ebony shapes beneath the beam of the searchlight from the pilot house. Canoeing the Mississippi suddenly seemed a good thing.

For the next couple of days things went astonishingly well. We had a luxurious hotel night in La Crosse, Wisconsin, where they told us how the French had named an Indian game after the shape of the stick used in it - first La Croix, then La Crosse, both the game and, eventually, the town. The main centre for an extensive agricultural area it was substantially bigger than Winona, but here too there were few traces to be seen of the golden era of lumbering and steamboats. But here there were new industries to absorb the displaced sawmill hands when lumbering died and La Crosse was one of the few riverside towns that didn't suffer a major slump. It had been a big shipbuilding centre too, till the rail bridges were built across the Mississippi and the steamboats were gradually

33

pushed out of business. But they still had a replica sternwheeler chugging up and down the river on sightseeing trips. "And we still build them for export to the tourist places in other States," our guide from the tourist office told us.

A few miles south of La Crosse, the sloughs opened out into a wide pool that presaged the next lock and dam on the Wisconsin shore. There was absolutely no doubt that the fastest route was by the navigation channel, but it was equally certain that with the winds in their current mood we'd be in for a precarious ride as the channel swung from the Minnesota to the Wisconsin shore. At this point the pool was 3 miles wide and broken only by a handful of sandbanks and islets, most of which had disappeared anyway under waters now swollen, and still rising, after rains almost unprecedented for the month of June.

Back in Winona, our friends at the Wildlife Refuge had agreed with George's idea of following the Minnesota shore and portaging into Reno Bottoms, a maze of sloughs appearing on our charts like one of those mind-twisting puzzles with which children and psychiatrists delight in testing our mental agility.

"If you follow Running Slough," Glen Sherwood had said, tracing it with his finger, "It'll take you into Pickerel Slough, then Minnesota Slough, and back into the navigation channel more or less straight down to Lansing. It's a real lonely area, but there are two or three recreational sites where you'll be able to camp."

Running Slough looked an appropriate name, for its blue thread roamed in every direction, occasionally coming to an apparent dead end; but everyone assured us that with the water so high, there'd be no problem in finding a way through.

We found an excellent unofficial camp site in a field near a tavern whose barmaid insisted on buying us drinks because she was "so happy to meet such interesting folk." But next morning it was a slow plod against headwinds through the sluggish waters of stump fields and shallows to our portage point. By mid-morning we were in Reno Bottoms. High water had injected the current with a welcome speed and we scurried for a while quite happily between the tangled cottonwoods and willows. The silence that contained them seemed primeval, and made only more so by the cries and calls, shrieks and warbles of bird and animal life that remained singularly invisible. Until "What on earth's that?" exclaimed George, and swung the canoe round.

Hunched on a tree stump a bird of enormous proportions glared at us unblinkingly. Consultation with our bird books confirmed it was a juvenile bald eagle and we lingered over its magnificence, proximity and lack of fear for some time.

Soon after that it began to rain, without wind this time - just a thin veil of steady rain of the most penetrating kind. Yet again we stowed away cameras and binoculars and struggled into ponchos. Judging from the leaden sky we were in for a long damp day.

One hour merged into the next in a grey all-pervading wetness through which discomfort gradually grew into a sense of unease. Insidiously, land was disappearing. There were clumps and parallel lines of trees, but the land on which they stood had simply vanished under spreading sheets of grey water, now dimpling and crumpling in the curtains of rain. High water had rendered the charts useless. Any doubts we'd had of our way being blocked were replaced by disquieting uncertainty amongst an endless choice of direction across unbroken water. Indeed, we changed direction so frequently that we no longer knew whether the bluffs so tantalisingly ahead were in Minnesota or Wisconsin. If the latter we were badly wrong; if the former they remained depressingly unattainable.

The rain increased in intensity and distant rolls of thunder brought a return of sickening fear. I kept remembering the warning repeated many times. "Don't get caught out on that river when the weather's mean." And now there was simply nowhere to go. I tried counting paddle strokes to steer my mind away from fear, inadequacy, weariness and a distressing awareness that, as an expedition partner, I was abysmally lacking in the essential qualities.

Then George remembered the compass he had brought as much out of habit as with any idea that we might need it. Getting a bearing in the soggy cramped conditions of the canoe was another matter, complicated by the unwieldy size of the charts, lack of visibility and spectacles astream with rain. But many years of experience of considerably worse conditions on mountains have given George an enviable talent to thrive on adversity. After a few curses he confidently announced where we were and in which direction we should be heading. Later he admitted the confidence was more assumed than real as he had no idea how far we had come. In the event he led us unfalteringly towards the first recreation site on the map.

We found it and its access road several feet under water that lapped gently over the picnic tables. A party of dripping fishermen were hauling their motorboat out of the water on a trailer clamped to a four-wheel drive truck. They plied us with coffee and offered to drive us to Lansing still 14 paddling miles ahead, but George would have none of it.

At least we had the comforting knowledge we were on the right side of the river. The next marked site was a mere couple of miles away but even with the compass we kept finding ourselves in lake-like areas that had no outlet other than the way we had come. When at last we reached it Visgers Landing turned out to be nothing more than an access point at the foot of steep bluffs. Immediately above it were the rail tracks of the Milwaukee Road, and above that the main road from which a dirt lane wound down to the landing and a small parking area for cars. Cold and sodden we unloaded our gear and battered our tent pegs into stony ground immediately beneath a "No Camping" sign. There was nowhere else to go.

Within our priceless aluminium box everything was bone dry. It is George's profoundly held belief that no one can fully appreciate the normal comforts of life until they have experienced the ultimate discomforts. With dry clothes, a hot meal inside us and solid ground under our feet, I could almost agree as long as I kept my thoughts off tomorrow. The rain let up for a brief interval and we strolled around our small domain before turning in.

The next storm broke soon after. It wasn't as alarming as the Great River Harbor episode in terms of wind or even thunder, but the volume of water that fell that night was beyond anything either of us had known. Even the creaks and squeaks of the mile-long cargo trains periodically grinding along the Milwaukee Road immediately above our heads were drowned by the clamorous tattoo on the flysheet. Neither of us slept much. Curled up in my sleeping bag I tried to explain the considerable doubts I had about my future part in the venture.

"It's quite abominable to be scared so much of the time. It may sound nonsense, but I've got the feeling this river is out to get me. You're different - meeting challenges is something you've always revelled in. But I don't know what I'm trying to prove or even if I want to prove anything. I know you've got to go on, but maybe we could find someone to take my place? We've met enough people who think it's a marvellous idea."

"Look," George said, "I don't want to 'go on' with anyone else. You're doing wonderfully. You're still remembering that Dordogne business, aren't you? But you'll forget about it in a few days, you'll see. Anyway, this sort of weather *can't* go on for ever."

Next morning a voice from Lansing announced from our little radio that $5\frac{1}{2}$" of rain had fallen in $3\frac{1}{2}$ hours that night. And there was more to come.

Chapter Three.
- *Of Rising Water and River Rats* -

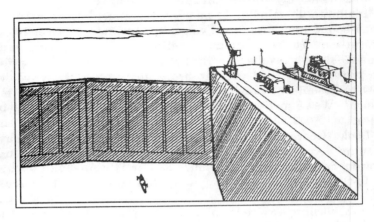

As we pulled away from the security of our scrappy little camp site next morning and headed out again into the flooded bottomlands, a sky weighed down with foreboding seemed to sit on the very tree tops. I found so much unalleviated greyness and the omnipresence of water unbelievably sinister and, as the rain started and a distant streak of fork lightning was followed by a long celestial growl, imagination began working overtime again.

The storm kept its distance, but the rain was soon steadily saturating. There was just one more chance of landing in the next 12 miles to Lansing and, on the charts, it looked a pretty straightforward run of four miles; but the high water had turned the route into a labyrinth and it became another compass job. I occupied my mind most of the time thinking up the most convincing arguments as to why, if and when we found the landing, we should make it our next camp. There was, of course, no possible justification after so short a distance unless cowardice qualified and, as a strengthening wind began to whip up the water, cowardice became a strong contender. But the decision was taken for me. When we reached New Albin Landing it was indeed a proper camp site, but the

Mississippi had got there first. The only corner above water was a small mound on top of which perched two dilapidated shacks housing the loos.

We paddled to the foot of it, glad to take the opportunity to stretch our legs, but I kept my thoughts of camping to myself.

Checking the charts, George observed "We're now in Iowa, our third State." "Seven to go," I calculated, but kept that thought to myself too.

Maybe the gods decided to reward such restraint or maybe they just took pity on their inadequate child. Anyway the rain stopped, the wind eased, the sky lightened, and before long we were back in the main channel. And all at once the world began to seem quite amazingly normal as motor launches and the occasional water skier dashed about, making the most of what had now materialised into a bright Sunday morning, and a tow plodded away into the distance. Gone was the eerie isolation and its ominous undertones. For the moment the Mississippi was once more just a big busy river on its way to the sea.

We made Lansing by lunch time. From an office that looked perilously close to the water a girl with blonde hair bounced out at our approach. "Say, you must be the British guys," she exclaimed. "They said on La Crosse radio to look out for that red canoe." Of course we could leave the canoe in her marina, and no there wouldn't be any charge. And we sure must have had a helluva time in that storm last night.

We nosed the We-no-nah in between a couple of motor cruisers and followed her into the office. With the bluffs rising almost from the river banks and barely space for the railway and road to squeeze past the single-storey houses along the water-front, camping prospects looked bleak.

"No camp site," agreed our new friend Valerie, "But there's a motel a few blocks out of town." We enquired how far, in rural terms, a few blocks might be. "About a mile I guess," She said. She seemed to take it for granted that she would drive us there and, as yet another deluge erupted as we were checking in, casually handed us the keys. "You'll need a car to get about; drop it back tomorrow. I can use my Dad's."

We could only stammer our thanks.

After a snack at Ma's and Pa's café, where most of the conversation centred on the number of cars carried away during the previous night's flash floods, we took a closer look at Lansing. There wasn't much of it, and what there was typified the many small communities whose lives had shrivelled when the railroad came and the steamboats departed. Between showers we watched some of their successors manoeuvring their huge rafts of barges under Lansing Bridge and round a 45 degree bend upstream of it, and drove up on to the bluffs to look down on our river. That evening as another storm crashed above our heads, blessed-ly muted by the security of four walls, we switched on the TV for the weather forecast.

"They certainly don't do things by halves," George commented as we watched a succession of animated graphs and charts, with a commentary about fronts and cloud cover and percentage chances of sun, storm or rain, delivered at breakneck speed. But we were fast learning why Americans are obsessed by their weather, and the message we unravelled seemed basically optimistic.

On our way to the marina next day we called on Margaret Anderson of the Wildlife and Fish Refuge. She was delighted to hear of our encounter with the juvenile bald eagle in the sloughs, having tagged it on the nest quite recently. We produced our charts and she marked on them more eagles' nests on our route that day.

The river had risen further in the night and at the marina we found Valerie looking worried, as well she might, for the water was only inches below her little office. "I've gotten a summer lease on this place," she explained. "And if the river keeps on rising I'm gonna have to move the office and the gas pumps." She cheered up. "But it looks pretty good today. You guys leaving now? It was great knowing you. Take care on that river."

We slipped across the main channel and away behind the islands in search of Margaret Anderson's bald eagles, and though we didn't find them, we saw gaudy woodcock and a group of turkey vultures riding the thermals with an elegance totally at odds with the appearance of these unappealing scavengers seen at close quarters. We could not, however, linger too long for a decision had to be made: whether or not to cross to the Wisconsin side of Pool Nine. If we stayed on the Iowa side, it would mean a portage over into Pool Ten and, more to the point, several miles of navigation through a network of sloughs on the other side. If we followed the more orthodox route through Lock 9, we would be obliged to change to the Wisconsin side across about three miles of exposed water. Neither of us was terribly attracted to another long section through swollen sloughs quite so soon. On the other hand though the day seemed to be fulfilling last night's prediction we suspected the general TV forecast, unlike that of local met. stations, was aimed at the land-bound. It had, for instance, made no reference to wind. Unusually that day it was a north-westerly, and it was freshening.

George left the decision to me. The charts did show a scattering of islands that might offer shelter on the long crossing, but most of them had disappeared under high water. All the same I knew what the decision must be. If I were not to continue indefinitely succumbing to my own fears and retrieve a degree of self-respect, I just had to come to terms with this river. "We'll cross," I said.

Initially we were in the shallow water of stump fields and with the wind coming obliquely from behind we bucketed uncomfortably towards the first of the visible islands about a mile away. As we turned along its leeward shore there was an interlude of calm before we came out into more exposed and deep water and into turbulence that was not nice at all. So the smooth continued to alternate with the increasingly agitated as, at a snail's pace, we pulled closer to Wisconsin's bluffs. It took about an hour, I didn't like it one bit, but at least I managed not to say so, even when George said "Well done. That wasn't so bad was it?"

The wind pretty well blew us down to Lock 9, still buffeting us at an angle which made steering difficult for George and sent the bows, and me in them, bobbing and swaying. At last in the calm of the lock chamber I allowed myself just a modicum of self-satisfaction and the faint hope that we might learn to live with each other, the Mississippi and I.

About a mile down river, the commercial camp site recommended by the lockmaster proved to be a collection of mobile homes and caravans, officially not available to such water gipsies as us. Fortunately the few occupants seemed delighted to accommodate us, for much of it was under water and what remained must have been the only available dry land for a very long way along that narrow strip between the river and the Burlington Northern. Throughout the night the wails and creaks of the latter periodically drowned the chorus of tree frogs that started up as soon as darkness fell.

We were now within easy striking distance of Prairie du Chien and the rare prospect of two nights in one place. By now we had evolved a most effective procedure for establishing local contacts, the unexpected reward for our perseverence with often frustrating correspondence during eighteen months of planning. In most cases the response, if any, had yielded little more than a name and a telephone number, acquired from State or local tourist departments, sometimes accompanied by a batch of leaflets on the local sights. Such letters as we received were mostly cautious in content, if not downright discouraging.

The warm response to our first tentative telephone call announcing our probable arrival in Winona on a certain day had come as a very welcome surprise. And so it had continued. It wasn't until well into our journey that one of our lengthening chain of new friends explained "We get all kinds of folk writing in with some crazy plan. They've just read Tom Sawyer or seen some TV programme, and the next thing they're all set to come down the Big Muddy in a rubber dinghy or on a raft or in a barrel. Most of 'em never turn up; some do and get into trouble and someone has to fish 'em out. Sometimes they've never even been on the water, let alone on a mean old river like this one, but they just got to thinking it would be a nice idea. So we're kinda cautious until we know more about the set-up."

We had called Prairie du Chien from La Crosse. "I'm so happy to have your call," announced someone called Nancy, and sounded it. "Keep to the main channel and near the bridge you'll see a park and a small landing place. Leave the canoe and come on up to the Rose Gordon Tavern and call us from there."

So after a trouble-free morning's paddling we did go on up to the Rose Gordon Tavern, situated on a largeish low lying island. Now linked by bridges to the rest of Prairie this was the oldest part of town where traces of the early 19th century Fort Crawford and a number of later 19th century buildings survived. It was also the most vulnerable area to flood. While we awaited the arrival of our welcoming committee we studied a display on the tavern walls which smartly put our own little problems with high water into perspective. Photographs of streets deep under water and the shambles of the aftermath showed the reality of life in a riverside town when the Mississippi was truly in flood.

"Yeah, she rises 'most every May" the barman said. "Then about every ten years we get a real flood. That means 21, 22 feet which brings her up to the steps here. When she gets to 25 feet it's time to leave. Now? Oh, she's around 14 feet, and that's kinda strange for June."

The Corps of Engineers and the city fathers planned to move all the remaining inhabitants off the island. Most had gone already, but the occupants of the Rose Gordon were standing firm. "There's been a tavern here since 1820; they'll have to bring in the Marines to shift us."

Later Nancy, a lively lass from the Convention and Visitors Bureau, took us to see the sights, one of them being a bearded, colourful character called Don Valley, the sole surviving full-time commercial fisherman on that section of the river. On our approach to Prairie we had already noted a number of curious square-ended, flat-bottomed vessels with what appeared to be a pair of bed rails fixed to the deck. Now Don explained that the vessels were clamboats and the "bed rails" bars from which hung rows of chain lengths, each bearing several hooks at the end. The bars were lowered over the side of the boat as it slowly drifted over a bed of clams in the Mississippi mud and soon after was raised again, hopefully with a clam clinging tenaciously to every hook. And so the procedure was repeated.

Thus in the 1890s Prairie was among many riverside towns

on the Upper Mississippi which boosted its lumber economy with the production of one very commonplace item. It was a German immigrant in Muscatine, Iowa, who first noticed the similarity between the shell of the Mississippi clam and the horn from which he had produced buttons back in his native country. Within a couple of years, the pearl button "rush" was on. From makeshift beginnings in ramshackle sheds with primitive equipment, button factories with more sophisticated machinery had burgeoned along the river banks and, from them, buttons in their multi-millions had poured out from the Midwest to the haberdasheries and fashion houses of the world. Processing involved first cooking the clams to separate shells from meat, the latter now destined as hog food, fertiliser or fish bait. A rare bonus might be the discovery of a pearl.

Later, as we progressed down river it was easy enough to recognise some of the one-time "button" towns by their beaches of discarded clam shells, every one perforated with neat round holes. But the factories had long since gone for the development of plastic heralded the demise of the pearl button soon after World War II. So why were they clamming now?

The answer lay in another enterprise not far from the Rose Gordon Tavern on the banks of the river. Here the Tennessee Shell Co. processed a million tons of clam shells annually for dispatch to Tennessee where they were ground into pellets for export to Japan's cultured pearl industry. And no doubt, Don agreed, a substantial percentage of that production subsequently found its way back again to North America.

When he wasn't clamming Don was harvesting the Mississippi for more edible fare like carp, catfish, buffalo and sheepshead, which were loaded on to refrigerated trucks twice a week for the dinner tables of Chicago. The law forbad the commercial selling of locally caught game fish, so such delicacies as walleye, crappie, sunfish that dominated many riverside restaurant menus had more distant origins. Don was not optimistic about the current fishing scene though. "Just ain't what it used to be," he said ruefully. "Them locks and dams may be good for navigation, but they're no darned good for me."

Before we left Nancy drove us across the bridge to Pike's Peak in Iowa where, high up on the bluffs, we looked down on the reason for Prairie's beginnings: the junction of Wisconsin river with the Mississippi. Just over 300 years ago, in a vessel not so very different from ours, Father James Marquette and Louis Joliet had nosed their way into the Big Muddy at the end of that first exploratory journey from the Great Lakes and became the first white men to set eyes on the Upper Mississippi. For the Indians whose ancestral mounds peppered the hill tops all round, life was never the same again. When the French traders later followed, poling their flat boats against the Mississippi current from as far away as New Orleans, they brought guns, tools and liquor to exchange for pelts, and the eventual fate of Indian culture was sealed.

In the interpretative centre of the nearby Effigy Mounds National Park, we watched a film about the mounds now protected within the Park's boundaries - nearly 200 of them, some painstakingly created in the form of bears or birds. Experts still wrangle over their meaning and function; some are undoubtedly burial mounds or territorial markers, others possibly the focus of rituals closely connected with the natural forces which dominated the annual cycle of Indian life. Whatever their purpose such mounds from a succession of cultures stretching back over 2000 years once dotted the landscapes of America in their multi-thousands. Most have been flattened for farm land or buildings.

"I guess they were managing better on their own," Nancy said thoughtfully. And I guessed she was right.

Conditions were ideal next morning and despite a fairly late start we made nearly 20 miles, alternating between minor sloughs and the main channel, and camping that evening within sight of Lock and Dam 10 at Guttenberg. A full size tow beat us to it by a short head next morning so we left the canoe in a backwater and went off to enquire of the lockmaster when we might expect to go through.

"I've another tow coming up after this, but I'll tell him to hold back. I'll be ready for you in around an hour and a half." As we thanked him and turned away he called after us. "They've been asking after you at Lock 11 - I'll tell 'em you're on your way. Oh, and there's a lady looking for you." The bush telegraph was obviously working well.

We found her sitting at the top of the steps looking down at our canoe. "I guessed you might like some news from home," she said handing us a copy of the Weekly Guardian from Britain. "But really I just wanted to hear a British accent. I'm Shirley Kellogg, by the way. My husband edits the local paper, and I'm supposed to interview you."

It was a nice small town, busy smartening up its disused brick and stone-built warehouses into little boutiques and craft workshops. With a name like Guttenberg it hardly came as a surprise that the place had been founded by German immigrants. We didn't, however, expect it to justify its famous association with the very earliest days of the printed word until Shirley took us to the newspaper office in which was proudly displayed a facsimile of the Guttenberg Bible, acquired by the paper's proprietor while serving in Germany in the 1940s.

Everything went our way for the next three days: a brisk current, sunshine, windless conditions, and no alarming wide pools to be crossed. The only continuing problem was finding dry land. With local advice we pinpointed an apparently ideal camp site on the Wisconsin shore, and the extremely complex route by which to reach it. In a canoe it is highly desirable to be very precise about directions. Bungling the right entrance to a network of sloughs can mean a hard paddle back against the current - too hard for any distance more than a few hundred yards with our load and the current as it was.

It was with a great sense of triumph, therefore, that we found the camp site - and with a corresponding sense of dismay surveyed the several inches of water lapping over it. Beyond was a tangle of willow and cottonwood with the bluffs rising out of it. We paddled as far as possible up the flooded gravel access road, then followed it on foot, clambering over the railway line and on a quarter of a mile to the welcome sight of a scattering of houses. At first they all seemed empty, but with some relief we came upon a cluster of mobile homes and signs of life in a building that announced itself as the Far Nuf Tavern.

"No shoes, no shirts, no service," warned the usual notice on the door but the owner, Bob Cook, and the little group propping up the bar were too astonished by our accents and our provenance to be worried by George's bare chest. Bob immediately put his truck at our disposal to collect any necessary gear from the canoe. "You won't need the tent," he added. "You can have one of my trailers - I guess you could use a shower."

A splendid old man in a Stetson and overalls couldn't get over it. "Why, there's folks lived all their lives around here who get lost looking for those cuts from the main river. Isn't that just something!" It was enormously good for our egos, as was the remainder of that convivial evening as we gnawed on succulent barbecued spare ribs and news of our deeds was conveyed to every new arrival.

A couple of days later the Mississippi decided we'd had, for the moment, our ration of trouble-free travel. We had spent the night at an official site back on the Iowa shore and were breaking camp when cars and trailers began pouring in, bearing a considerable fleet of canoes. Emerging from a police car the imposing figure of the local Deputy Sheriff explained that a triathlon of canoeing, cycling and running was about to begin.

It was a glorious early morning and when we discovered We-no-nah canoes much in evidence, along with some of the canoe fraternity we had planned to contact in Dubuque the next day, the temptation to linger was too much. We watched them set off for a two and a half mile upstream paddle and waited for the leaders to return and leap on their bicycles before setting off ourselves.

The delay proved a big mistake. As had happened so often a whiff of breeze began to ruffle the calm morning, and by the time we were approaching Lock and Dam 11 a vicious north-easterly was sending ridges of white-caps racing across the wide open expanses of Pool 11. We needed to be on the Iowa shore because of the lock but in all other respects it was the wrong side to be. Out on the open water the turbulence was horrific, but if we stayed too close to the steep rocky shore there was every risk of being dashed against it. Ahead of us a long dyke jutted out from the shore. To get into the lock we would have to pull round it and out into the open pool. Having done so there was no knowing if we might have a long wait for barges locking through from downstream, and

I began to appreciate why some of our predecessors had equipped themselves not only with an engine but also with a two-way radio. The sick fears I had almost forgotten in recent days surged back.

"This bloody, bloody river," I wailed. "What the hell are we going to do?"

The only feasible alternative was to land. Bouncing like a cork and buffeted almost uncontrollably by wind and waves, the canoe careered towards the rocky dyke. And there the expedition might have come to an untimely end if George had not somehow managed to steer us into an unsavoury soup of driftwood and other flotsam driven by the same conditions into the angle between dyke and shore. By dint of huge effort we managed to jam the canoe far enough into this soggy jumble to be beyond the turbulence, hauled ourselves within reach of land and scrambled ashore. It was an awful place. The banks were almost perpendicular and entirely composed of jagged rocks covered with a tangle of bushes and brambles. Immediately above ran the railway at the foot of sheer bluffs. The only possibility was to hump our equipment up the bank, along the railway and down on to the other side of the dyke where a relatively sheltered backwater opened out on to the lock approaches.

It took us an hour and a fair collection of scratches and bruises to complete the portage, and another half hour to ease the empty canoe close enough to the dyke to lift it across. By the time we had re-loaded, a couple of small motor launches had joined us in the shelter of the backwater to await instruction for locking though. Even now we had to manoeuvre out into pretty stormy waters to get into the lock itself, and it remains a miracle how we didn't turn over in the process.

A mile below the lock two figures waved wildly at us from the top of the levee and signalled us into the blessed calm of a marina, where local TV and radio reporters were poised to record our bedraggled arrival.

By an odd geological quirk Dubuque owed its birth, development and initial prosperity to lead. In the 1780s, pursuing rumours of rich lead deposits the French-Canadian Julien Dubuque paddled his canoe into Catfish Creek, just south of the present town, and established one of the earliest permanent settlements west of the Mississippi. Those were the days, our guide reminded us, when today's Midwest was yesterday's Northwest. Minneapolis was still a wilderness wasteland, the source of the Mississippi had yet to be discovered. On the basis of a rare relationship of mutual respect the local Fox Indians granted Dubuque rights to work their lead mines. When he died in 1810 they reverted to the Indians, but not for long. Decimated by the blood-bath of the Black Hawk War the Indians relinquished all their territorial rights in the area in 1833, and the white settlers flooded in.

That was the year modern Dubuque was born, and the first lumber rafts landed. When lead declined Dubuque diversified into lumber, farming and meat packing, and continued to flourish rather better than most, even benefiting from the arrival of the railroad. Modern industry, like the mammoth John Deere agricultural machinery plant, shifted the focus away from the river. All the same we found plenty of nostalgic echoes among the ornate residences of the lead and lumber barons up on the bluffs, and in the older business districts along Main and Locust Streets behind the downtown warehouse area on the river shore.

Some of the warehouses had been restored and housed craft shops and exhibitions and in the harbour, across the rail lines, the *William M. Black*, a vintage 1934 sidewheeler, served as part of a rather good Riverboat Museum. Alongside, the replica stern-wheeler *Spirit of Dubuque* operated by day as a sightseeing boat, by night as a floating restaurant. You couldn't deny that downtown Dubuque was trying very hard.

Our next port of call, Galena, lay a brisk day's paddling downstream. "You may stay in a nearby four-star resort or, if you prefer, with some River Rat friends I know," Donald Jonjack, Curator of the Galena Historical Museum, had written in one of the rare replies we received to our avalanche of letters. He went on to explain that Galena was the most important port on the Upper Mississippi in the mid-19th century. An accompanying leaflet announced that Galena was the best-preserved 19th century town in America.

Galena, like Dubuque, had been born of lead, but there the resemblance ended. To begin with it wasn't even on the Mississippi, but four miles up the little Galena river. By another masterly piece of navigation George found its mouth tucked away behind a maze of islands, on the way crossing in to Illinois, our fourth State. Now largely silted up, it was hard to believe that this modest milky green waterway, burrowing through a tunnel of silver maple, was once a bustling highway for paddle steamers in their scores. All the same the current it produced was quite strong enough for those sufficiently daft to canoe against it.

We had opted for the River Rats whoever they might be, and indeed their motorboat caught up with us just as we were rounding the last bend. "Hi! We've been out looking for you," they shouted, tossing a can of beer at George and exuding the same sort of scatty energy as boisterous, friendly puppies.

"They've talked about nothing else but your coming," Don Jonjack told us later. It had been decided that we should spend our second night with them at their "headquarters", known as Camp 19. "I guess you're living their most cherished dream. But they're a nice bunch - a bit laid back, maybe, but nice. They'll give you a good time."

We drove round the steeply up-and-down little town with Don and his wife Janet, and found it wholly delightful. In view of later events there was a rather bitter irony in Julien Dubuque's success in encouraging some of his Indian friends to switch from their traditional hunting economy to mining and smelting. Thus a number of their primitive furnaces were operating in the Galena area by the time the first mining lease was granted to a white settler by the Federal Government in 1822. In the same year the first steamboat also reached the upper Mississippi.

"After that the whole place was soon crawling with folk prospecting and digging," Don said. "They came from all over, many of 'em from other parts of the States, but others direct from Europe, especially the English and Irish and, later, the Germans." George, whose antecedents hailed from the lead-mining valleys of the Yorkshire Dales, was fascinated to find twice as many Spenceleys in the Galena telephone directory

50

as in London's.

Inevitably skirmishes with the resident Indians resulted, but the Black Hawk War put an end to that. By 1845, annual lead production peaked at over 54 million lbs - 80% of the nation's lead supply - and thirty steamers were working regularly out of Galena, each towing a string of keelboats loaded with ore and the wheat produced by pioneer farmers who had moved in following the expulsion of the Indians.

"It's hard to realise now that back in the 1840s and '50s, when Chicago was just a couple of mud huts, this was about the most important city in the West," Don mused. And like all frontier towns it had been "wide open": a human conglomerate of the new-rich with their social aspirations, the hard-headed, the rowdy, unscrupulous and unruly. One visitor in 1837 recorded in his diary "Much vice and dissipation going on" and spoke of the gaming house in which "numbers are nightly and daily fleeced."

By 1857, the population had swollen to 12,000, but the economic slither was already well under way. Lead production was on the decline, experienced miners had packed up their tools to follow bigger dreams in the gold fields of California, and the river was getting visibly narrower and shallower by the year.

"And almost as though they were set on their own self-destruction," Don added, "the city fathers stubbornly rejected an approach from the railroad company to bridge the Mississippi from close by Galena. So they took it up river and carried it across to Dubuque instead, and after that I guess Galena was pretty well doomed."

The town's final historical act was to provide the Union Army with no less than nine generals during the Civil War. Among them was General Ulysses S. Grant who was wildly fêted on his victorious return. The house built as Galena's gift to the General and other gracious old homes were high among the town's tourist attractions. For somewhere along the line, the Midwest had become aware that it was harbouring a little gem - a backwaters community completely overlooked by the speculators and developers and, therefore, a virtually untouched relic of 19th century America. Artists and craftsmen began to flock there, and the tourists followed. In all our journey through the Midwest, the only foreign visitors we met - a group of Japanese - were in Galena. Old stores and warehouses suddenly turned into studios and wineries. Gracious old homes opened up for bed and breakfast. We stayed in one of them that first night, up on the hill, looking out at another wild storm as tornado warnings crackled out over the radio, thankful not to be on the river.

Americans who knew Europe would break off wryly as they began to enthuse about some ancient building all of 50 years old. But Galena's could clock up a respectable 100-150 years and there was something very appealing about the extravaganza of architectural styles that somehow combined an almost aggressive individualism with confused Old World nostalgia. Thus in a profusion of cornices and friezes, belvederes and cupolas, pilasters and pediments, gables and dormers, they encapsulated a couple of milennia of styles successively described as Greek Revival, Gothic Revival, Italianate, Romanesque Revival, Second Empire and Queen Anne.

The next evening our River Rat friends loaded our canoe on to one of their motorboats and bore us triumphantly down to Camp 19. It was a ramshackle house on stilts on the shore of an island looking out over the main channel of the Mississippi, the front of it almost completely hidden behind a huge White Ensign, purloined in our honour from a source we could not begin to imagine. They explained that Camp 19 had originally been started in 1895 by 19 men of Galena as a social club. Rebuilt in 1915, it was now the River Rats' cherished bolthole to which they escaped at every opportunity. But its days were numbered.

"Our lease is up come two years," one of them said sombrely. "Then they'll want us out."

"They?"

"Corps of Engineers. Raising the water level and stuff like that. Folks like us are inconvenient when they want to mess about with the river. We're gonna litigate." I found myself hoping they would win, but doubting it.

The yard was well under water; indeed the river came lapping half way up the steps to the porch. Nobody minded. The girls got busy preparing salads. The men settled down to drinking beer. One of them, Patrick, who worked in a screen printing shop when he wasn't being a River Rat, was in charge of cooking sausages over a charcoal grill fixed to a rickety cylinder out in the flooded yard. I sloshed around watching him and the antics of a pair of belted kingfishers.

"What exactly is a River Rat?" I asked.

"I guess it's just someone who loves the river, spends every moment they can by or on her." Patrick prodded the sausages, and grinned at me. "I guess that's what *you* are."

"Sometimes I'm scared silly out there," I confessed.

"It's the folks that aren't that get into trouble. You've got to be respectful. But just look how beautiful she is now."

And she was. We sat late into the evening watching the day die and the river turn silver and black, and later the fire flies filling the dark with their winking lights. Some of the River Rats had to return to Galena that night, reluctantly responding to the demands of jobs and normal life. We watched their navigation lights disappear and heard the sound of their engines merge into the restless quiet of the river. Next morning those that remained helped us get on our way.

Patrick said, "A little part of us will be travelling with you from now on. We won't add to the weight, but we'll be there..."

Chapter Four.
"The Brits are back"

Highwater conditions obliged us to make use of offical camp sites on the Illinois bank for the following two nights. Both were accessible by road and our fellow campers were all motorised producing between them an impressive array of caravans, trailers and what George called jousting tents, his idea of a true tent being one that you have to crawl in to. Ours certainly looked the odd one out and attracted a good deal of friendly interest.

One of the sites was beneath the towering limestone bluffs that dominated Pallisades State Park, one of whose wardens drove us to several viewpoints for rare eagle-eye views. The sun was setting and the swollen waters far below glinted azure and black, purple and pink. This much had not changed since Mark Twain over a century earlier commented on the extraordinary sunsets of the Upper Mississippi.

"Not much sign of all those sand bars we were promised would make such splendid camp sites," I commented. Indeed you could have counted them on the fingers of one hand in the three weeks since the night our tent blew down on one below Lake Pepin.

"Presumably there won't be too many more of these either,"

said George, waving an arm at the bluffs.

In the back of my log book I had pasted a folded strip of map, cut out from an atlas, showing the full length of the Mississippi. It had become a cherished daily task to record on it our progress. Despite its small scale even our shortest journeys made a visible impression, albeit only in millimetres.

That evening I studied the map more closely, reminded now that we were soon to reach a significant stage of the journey. The topographical pattern of the river with its labyrinth of sloughs opening out into wide pools above each lock-and-dam had become an established part of our lives. So had the twin rims of the bluffs hemming our horizons at a greater or lesser distance from either shore. It was difficult to imagine it would ever change. Yet quite soon now, beyond the centimetre or so on my map that represented the next 60 miles, Rock Island would mark the end of the Mississippi Wildlife and Fish Refuge that had occupied all the islands and much of the uninhabited shores for nearly 300 miles. There would certainly be changes ahead.

In the meantime Clinton, Iowa was our next major port of call and our arrival there coincided with two significant events. The first was the town's Riverboat Days, a four-day bonanza culminating with the Fourth of July; the second was an invasion of mayflies.

A couple of hundred miles earlier a policeman in Wisconsin had forewarned us of these Midwest phenomena called mayflies, shadflies or, obscurely, Mormon flies, according to where you were. Overnight, it seemed, they hatched in their millions, filled the air with their aimless flutterings, mated and then died, leaving in their wake a stench of fish and layers of corpses that could be several inches thick.

"When they're real bad," our policeman friend had told us, "they gotta bring the snow ploughs out to clear the highway else the traffic's sliding every which way, like it's ice. I've seen some real terrible shadfly pile-ups."

First signs of the invasion had begun that morning as we broke camp and the resident red-headed woodpeckers were having a field day. Fortunately the mayflies showed a preference for land, but as the day progressed so did the messy rafts of their corpses increase on the water. When we reached Clinton the white superstructure of its Showboat - an old coal-fired Ohio river sternwheeler that served as museum - was almost hidden under a black layer of the wretched creatures, imminently to depart into some mayfly afterlife.

No one was taking too much notice of them on the riverside meadow beyond the levee where, amidst a sea of tents, stalls, side-shows and drifting balloons, milling humanity nibbled popcorn, sucked at cans of Coke or beer, or buried their noses in candyfloss. Stalls were piled with Stetsons and gaudy souvenirs and on the way to the Information Marquee we passed hopefuls hurling missiles at a weighted platform with the aim of plunging a young bathing beauty into a tank of water. Inside the marquee Jenny, our local contact, was deftly fielding a barrage of questions. "Hi!" she said. "Glad you made it. I've fixed up for you guys to camp with the Confederate Army."

And so she had. A few minutes later she took us over to a group of tents where we stepped straight back into the 1860s as appropriately dressed members of the Scotts Tennessee Artillery Company B, their womenfolk and children, enjoyed a brief respite before battle. A line of cannon and mortar were already in place, aimed across the meadow at the Unionist Camp a couple of hundred yards away.

An officer saluted us smartly. "Lootenant John Marsh at your service, sir, ma'am. We bid you welcome to our humble camp and it will be our endeavour to make your sojourn as comfortable as circumstances permit." But he couldn't keep it up. The Lieutenant, alias Bruce Kindig, a history teacher from Davenport, grinned hugely and relaxed.

Civil War Enactment groups, we discovered, were as much a part of the American way of life as folkloric ensembles were in Europe. Sometimes events lasted several days during which Civil War battles were re-enacted almost down to the last simulated casualty. As part of the more general festivities of Riverboat Days the present groups were just putting on a bit of a show, but costumes, weaponry, life style were still as authentic as possible. There really had been a Scotts Tennessee Artillery Company B and a Lieutenant John Marsh, Bruce assured us as he took us to meet some of the rest of the Company and their hangers-on.

In various parts of the camp a blacksmith was hammering, women stitched at uniforms and cannon balls were being "manufactured" from beer cans filled with flour and wrapped in tin-foil. A young woman, a small boy clinging to her hooped skirts, was examining a sutler's wares. And over a camp fire, acting cook Private John O'Donnell - alias Ed Reiter, a civil servant also from Davenport - was preparing grits, Johnny cakes and coffee.

"If it isn't the devil of an honour to greet our friends from across the water," he announced in an impeccable brogue, before embarking on a long and detailed account of how he had left Ireland in 1844 and of his subsequent service and wounds acquired in the war with Mexico. They continued to regale us with stories of their exploits, historical and modern. Later in the day the opposing armies fired noisily at each other, but in the evening there was a good deal of fraternising and we spent much of it sharing succulent barbecued steaks over at the Unionist camp, and swapping yarns by their camp fire. Our sleep was shattered next morning by the bugle blast of reveille.

The Mississippi was in a quiet mood when we returned to her after an excellent Confederate breakfast, and we slipped pleasantly through a series of sloughs with names like Beaver, Sunfish and Steamboat, featuring a couple of small lakes and a busily occupied heronry. By lunch time we were back in the main river and reached the marina at Camanche to be exuberantly welcomed by some of the canoeing fraternity met earlier in Dubuque. They had just completed a canoe race as part of Clinton's Riverboat Days and now swarmed down to the jetty bearing two enormous trophies. Unknowingly we had also just completed the same course and become the uncontested winners of the over-40s section.

It was a Sunday. That afternoon it seemed as though most of the population of the Midwest had taken to the river and it was not a comfortable experience. Earlier encounters with the weekend pleasure boat brigade had not endeared them to us, but now their numbers seemed almost menacing. The river, ironically in calm mood, fidgeted irritably as motor boats of every shape and size careered up and down, often passing far too fast and far too close to us, their occupants waving in happy ignorance of the discomfort and, at times, danger they were creating. In most circumstances we could ride the wash of a motorised vessel easily enough by pointing the bows into it at right angles; but when the wash was both high and close and combined with a general agitation, conditions became pretty unpleasant. The water skiers and their towing craft were the worst. George tried shouting and signalling at them, and then resorted to shaking his fists, but they only shouted and waved gaily back, assuming his gesticulations were in greeting.

By the time we reached the little community of Princeton we had had enough. "Ain't nowhere to camp in town," the marina owner said. "But you're welcome to put a tent up here." "Here" was a small patch of hard ground between the marina office and jetty. It was Hobson's choice and we accepted gratefully.

Way up river, a high sand bank on the opposite shore was covered with little black dots which, through our binoculars, we identified as people. So these were the sand parties we'd heard about when everyone roared off for a day "back to nature", well supplied with transistor radios and crates of beer. It accounted for the erratic behaviour of some of the river users that day, and later we learned from the Coast Guard that the combination of drinking and driving was just as much a killer on the river as on the roads. Soon after a stationary small boat was capsized in a surge of wash from a larger one that approached the marina jetty on full throttle. The occupants were fished out wet, shaken but unharmed; but it was a lesson on how easily accidents occur.

"This," said George, "is presumably the build-up to the Fourth of July. That's one day we'll keep right off this river."

The comings and goings of motor boats and the succession of cars backing down the ramp to haul them ashore went on far into the evening. Our "camp site" was a favourite gathering place for the occupants to down a last few beers and enthuse over the day's activities before heading for home. We waited till most of the traffic had died before pitching the tent. Darkness came and from the distant sand bank a quite impressive display of fireworks crackled and sparkled over the river. Returning motor boats and revellers punctuated the night. We slept fitfully as they stomped about, their transistors blaring a few feet from our heads.

The following day we were scheduled to reach the Quad Cities, a quartet of communities composed of Davenport and Bettendorf in Iowa, and Rock Island and Moline in Illinois. Everyone had been very discouraging about them. "Industrial... nothing to see... no point in stopping" was the general gist of opinions. Now it looked as though we would be obliged to accord them an extra day if we were to keep off the river on the Fourth of July.

Our approach to the Quad Cities did not augur well. The heat was tremendous and the current minimal. From Le Claire marina we rang through to Lock 14 to check there would be no delay.

Had we remembered some of our earlier readings we might have had a twinge of misgiving even on this windless day, for the 15 miles from Le Claire to Rock Island once formed a continuous rapid - the longest of the entire river and the most treacherous of its stretches of navigation. In the steamboat heyday goods were either trans-shipped through this section by local cargo haulers or guided through the chaos of rocks and eddies by one of an elite band of pilots. It was not until well after the Civil War that the most formidable rocks were removed and only in 1907 that the Mississippi's first lock at Moline finally made the rapids a hazard of the past.

But even had we remembered all this, our knowledge of the Corps of Engineers' efficient lock-and-dam system would probably have made it seem irrelevant. True there was, unusually, a separate smaller auxiliary lock for pleasure craft which might have struck us as significant. In the event we had checked that it was only in operation at weekends and therefore headed without any undue expectations for the main lock.

The river on its approaches was a model of benign calm. A motor boat joined us during the brief wait while a handful of small vessels were locked through from downstream. The lock gates opened to disgorge its occupants. From one launch a young man cupped his hands over his mouth and bawled "Look out. It's *rough* the other side!"

Once inside the lock chamber we made enquiries. "Yeah," said one of the lock hands. "The sluice gates are open and I guess it's kinda rough for a canoe." "We've had open sluice gates before," George said.

We had got into a bad habit of leaving off our life jackets as the weather became hotter, but now I insisted that we put them on. As the downstream lock gates slowly opened a scene of total turmoil was revealed. My heart plummeted. The motor boat that had shared the lock with us went ahead, tossed from one seething furrow to the next. George estimated later that the waves were four or five feet high. Fanning out from the open sluice gates they raced obliquely at us, catching us half side-on, crashing against the guide wall beyond the lock gates, and bouncing back to batter us from another angle.

With the greatest difficulty we kept ourselves away from the wall, but that was about the only manoeuvre we could attempt. The We-no-nah bucked and bounced, lurching from side to side at angles that seemed to defy all natural laws. A houseboat approaching the lock from downstream took one look at us and turned tail. I paddled with every ounce of strength I possessed and frankly prayed, and slowly we inched towards the end of the guide wall. Behind us we heard a faint cheer.

Once past it and the worst of the danger all I wanted was to feel solid land under my feet, but the river continued to seethe angrily for a couple of miles bearing us along at a speed that made even the prospect of landing seem unappealing. Even beyond that the currents were extremely odd as we edged past barge terminals, cement works and other industrial paraphernalia that signalled our approach to the Quad Cities.

Never had a place seemed more desirable. At last we reached the blessed haven of Lindsay's Boat Harbor where I clambered out, my knees like jelly, to be greeted by a photographer, a reporter and the cheery smile of Kay Paterson from the Chamber of Commerce.

Typical of the swings and roundabouts that had become a characteristic of our Mississippi journey, our three days in the Quad Cities were a delightful interlude. Kay, an attractive brunette Anglophile, was a charmer. "We're so *excited* about your visit," she said as though she meant it and, ignoring all protests, piled our most unsavoury belongings into her car "just to freshen things up a little". An hour later in the air-conditioned luxury of a baronial castle of a hotel near Bettendorf, we soaked away layers of tiredness and grime and, with it, the miserable fears of Lock 14.

Our informants had been only partially right. The Quad Cities were not beautiful but in river terms they played an interesting role and, in human terms, they did us proud. Kay and her friends took charge of us completely, quite genuinely thrilled that we were to have our first Fourth of July experience on their patch. "We'll do the Parade in East Moline, and the firework display in Bettendorf," planned Kay, "and there's a *lotta* history around here. Guess we're gonna wear you guys out."

At some point amidst the museums and art galleries and tours of elegant residential districts we had tea - cream cakes and a whole selection of tea bags to choose from - at Christie's in East Davenport whose mid to late 19th century houses were rapidly becoming restored into highly desirable properties. Across the water lay Rock Island, a notorious landmark in both the geography and history of the Mississippi. For the Indians it had been the revered home of a "Great and Good White Spirit", a place for fishing, hunting and religious ceremony. The White settlers put an end to that, ploughing up their sacred graves. Bitter conflict burgeoned into murder and pillage, and eventually the Blackhawk War of 1832, not the prettiest episode in American history.

For the Indians the ensuing treaty meant much more than the loss of vast tracts of land; it was the end of civilisation as they knew it. For the newcomers victory was followed by a phenomenal boom in the settlement of the Upper Mississippi. Mark Twain summed it up in a few sentences less than 50 years later, writing of "this amazing region, bristling with great towns, projected day before yesterday, so to speak, and built next morning." He went on to describe Davenport as "another beautiful city, crowning a hill - a phrase which applies to all these towns; for they are all comely, all well built, clean, orderly,

61

pleasant to the eye, and cheering to the spirit." It was too soon then to foresee the decay to be wrought by the decline and fall of river traffic, or the succession of booms and depressions that would follow.

Thirty years after the Blackhawk Treaty, Rock Island was playing its part in different war games. Today only a plaque marks the site of the notorious confederate Prison Camp in which, over a period of 20 months, nearly 13,000 prisoners were held. But we went to see the Confederate Cemetery where many of the 15% of them who died still lie at rest. The Unionist dead lie in a corner of the National Cemetery nearby.

With so much death associated with it, and despite Mark Twain's enthusiasm for the "charming island... the Government has turned into a wonderful park," it seemed appropriate that today Rock Island remains the home of America's biggest Arsenal, a-bristle with restrictions. Even the John M. Brown Memorial Museum, a favourite tourist sight, displays enough historic weaponry to equip a sizeable old-fashioned war.

We turned our attention to more lighthearted matters on the morning of the Fourth of July as we joined the crowds pouring in to East Moline and elbowed our way to where, in a store entrance, Kay and her friends from the Junior League had set up a stall. It was piled with T-shirts, peaked caps, buttons, stickers, all bearing the slogan "Quad Cities Joined by a River." There were also small bottles filled with cloudy contents labelled "Mississippi Water" at 50 cents a time. "All in a good cause," said Kay, noticing my raised eyebrows.

Main Street was packed with every generation and, above all, youngsters in holiday mood, sticky with candy floss, munching hotdogs or popcorn, waving balloons, perspiring profusely as the noonday temperature nudged steadily over the 95° F mark. It was already standing room only, every inch of kerb taken up by wriggling hordes of children and rows of chairs from which their elders observed them indulgently.

"It's an odd way to be celebrating our defeat," I mused, as the thought occurred to me for the first time.

Kay looked startled and then laughed. "I guess you are, too, But don't feel too bad about it."

"We should have put the canoe on a trailer and joined the Parade with a big banner 'Watch Out the Brits are Back'". She clapped her hands. "Oh, if only we'd thought of that in time." And just then the distant sound of a military band brought anticipation to fever pitch.

As it was we were presented by the Mayor with a T-shirt apiece and continued to celebrate our defeat in the utmost harmony as there unfolded before us in the hot, hot sun the amazing spectacle of a typical small town Fourth of July parade. Everyone who wasn't watching it, it seemed, was taking part in it.

For the best part of two hours floats and fire engines, tractors and trucks, vintage and veteran cars, stage coaches and bicycles, rolled slowly by. There were bagpipers and college and high school bands, little girls turning cartwheels, solemn small boys striding it out and, from a carriage, the Mothers of World War Two smiled self consciously. Banks and insurance companies, shops and factories, war veterans and youth groups and, not least, the politicians wooed us with slogans or vied for our attention with their displays. Cowboys rode into town, clowns darted among the young spectators, the Statue of Liberty passed solemnly on a trailer. Amidst them all trundled mammoth combine harvesters, like latter day dinosaurs, to represent this world capital of agricultural machinery, its dismal preoccupation with recessions momentarily forgotten. We ran out of film before the Parade was even half way through.

There was just time to freshen up at our hotel before setting off for the fireworks display. But first there was a phone call to make.

"Am I speaking to Lootenant John Marsh of the Scotts Tennessee Artillery company B?"

A pause. "Hi Sylvie. You and George hurry straight on over. We'll be firing the cannon in an hour."

So we joined our Confederate Army friends and their families in a Bettendorf park and, from its grassy slopes, heard their cannon signal trigger off the display of fireworks that exploded and cascaded in the night sky above the Mississippi as the Fourth of July reached a noisy finale for another year.

We were seen off the next morning by two television crews

and, by the time we had launched and covered the intervening mile, they were there again to immortalise our passage through Rock Island's Lock 15. Kay and her boss were there too, along with a gaggle of cheering school children and their teachers on an outing to the Lock's Visitors' Centre. We had observed that the sluice gates were open.

"How does it look the other side?" I yelled at Kay, preparing for the worst.

"Just fine," she shouted back. And so it was.

Above us soared the rail and highway bridge, successor to the first ever rail bridge to span the Mississippi in 1856. The steamboat captains obliged to trim their lofty stacks were incensed, Kay had told us. Within a year a vessel had hit the bridge and sunk, and the shipowners took up legal cudgels. But progress was not to be stemmed. Among the team of attorneys hired by the railroad company was one Abraham Lincoln. "One man has as good a right to cross the Mississippi as another to sail down it," he pronounced. And that was that.

So in our turn we continued to exercise the right apportioned to us and proceeded peacefully for the next three days. With Rock Island behind us we finally emerged from the Mississippi Wildlife and Fish Refuge. Gradually the character of the river scenery would change as the bluffs softened into wooded hills and rolling farmland. Most of the sloughs were now re-named chutes, usually broader and straighter, dividing islands that were mostly far more substantial than the humps of bottomlands forest further north. And for lengthening stretches there would be no islands at all.

At Fairport, Iowa, we made contact with George and Rita Koenigsaecker, a delightful couple whom we knew to be associated with the Great River Road. We were curious to know more about this landlubber's shadow of the Mississippi which likewise dissected the Continent from Lake Itasca to the Gulf of Mexico. But it proved to be a poor second best for there were vast sections, especially in the south, when the road was forced to retreat many miles from its Great River companion.

We met the Koenigsaeckers again next day a few miles downstream at Muscatine, the original home of the pearl button and still producing its polyester equivalent in considerable quantities. The town was called Bloomington until its inhabitants deemed the name too common and decided to become the world's unique Muscatine. And perhaps it still is.

The Davenport television crews had done their work effectively. "Was expecting you guys through yesterday," said the keeper of Lock 17, while at Keithburg's Lighthouse Restaurant they presented us with two River Rats T-shirts. In Campbell's Chute a plague of motor boats and water skiers were less impressed by our presence. George nearly came to blows with one of them as they roared through a "no-wake" area in a narrow stretch and nearly turned us over. "You think you own the f.....ing river?" bawled a paunchy specimen at the wheel of one motor boat and proceeded to repeat his highly dangerous manoeuvre. That was the night we were kept awake until the early hours by a whip-poor-will, a kind of nightjar with a mind-fraying habit of ceaselessly repeating its name, in this case only a few yards from our tent.

The weather men got it very wrong the next day, their promise of warmth and sunshine translated into a stiff south-easterly and a grey sky rapidly developing lowering thunder clouds. It was not too dismaying as we had risen early with the intention of breakfasting in Oquawka, less than six miles down river, mostly through sheltered waters. One of our predecessors had waxed enthusiastic about this little place, and especially, a particular tavern. It had obviously changed hands for it turned out to be a gloomy den full of fly-blown prints and dusty stuffed animals; but it served its purpose as the heavens discharged their next load.

The torrent eventually abated, but the wind did not. "Could be a rough ride," said a man docking his jonboat near our canoe. He glanced at the Union Jack on our bows. "You guys from Canada?" It was a better effort than many of our inquisitors who just could not "figure which State flag that could be." We made our confession and he said "well, I'll be goddarned."

We had taken a liking to the jonboat folk. As we eased southwards, there was a noticeable increase in the number of these flat-bottomed craft, powered by a simple outboard engine. For

65

the most part they were real river people using their modest vessels for fishing or simply getting from A to B; certainly not to be compared with the weekend pleasure boat brigade either for speed or ostentation and, least of all, for their ignorance of the river's ways, for almost unfailingly the jonboaters kept well clear of us or cut their engines if their curiosity got the better of them. Quite often in the weeks ahead they would go out of their way to pass the time of day with us, compare notes on the river and more than once give useful advice on their particular stretch of the Big Muddy.

There were a dozen miles and a lock to negotiate before our next stop at Burlington, Iowa. After a rather relaxed three days on the river I had a feeling the Mississippi was about to break our uneasy truce.

"Let's get this over," I said.

The thunder clouds had moved on but the south-easterly had strengthened into a steady gale. By hugging the shore it was not too bad for the bluffs of Illinois gave some protection, and we crept uneventfully if wearily down to Lock 18 to be rewarded by an immediate lock-through. It was then that a combined change of direction in the river and more exposed terrain began to create problems. We were still on the Illinois shore. Between us and Burlington on the Iowa side lay a series of islands threaded by sloughs; in order to reach them we needed to cross the navigation channel, now whipped up into ridges that surged against the current and at an oblique angle to the route we must take. We paused in a riverside park to take stock. George debated the possible advantages of the ferry glide.

"If we paddle like hell upstream," he said, "The wind will be more or less behind us, and with a bit of luck the current will carry us across to the islands."

I refrained from pointing out that the way this wind was blowing it would probably carry us lock, stock and barrel across the islands as well. Instead I simply said "Life jackets" and George did not argue.

It was unkind of fate to send along a tow and its great fleet of barges just at that moment. We sheltered behind a small island while it passed; but a distant smudge told us that yet another was imminent.

"Blast," George said. "Let's go or we'll be here for the rest of the day."

The mile-long trail of turmoil created by all passing towboats had not improved the situation. The surging and seething were frightful. Alternately praying, cursing and vowing that never again would I get back on this river once, and if ever, I got off it, I paddled with all my might. Yet even through my loathing and alarm I marvelled at the way our tiny craft once again defied all the fury that the river had unleashed on it. I reverted to an old habit of counting my paddle strokes with my eyes closed on the doubtful principle that you could not be afraid of what you could not see. At the best of times paddling upstream produces the unnerving sensation of standing still despite the most superhuman effort. When I reached 200 and re-opened my eyes, we had indeed barely moved either upstream or down; but the islands of Iowa with their sprinkling of summer houses were noticeably nearer, and I now kept my eyes open as the current ever so slowly nudged us closer to them.

At last we found respite in a back eddy. There were still four miles to go and the considerable task of edging down along the island to reach the more protected waters of sloughs, and then the final open stretch beneath a bridge into Burlington itself.

"I hate this river," I said. "I hate everything about it."

Even George was subdued. "We'll take it very easy, staying close to the shore. It'll be all right once we get behind the islands."

We nosed out of the back eddy and began bucketing our way along. It was a rocky shore and impossible to stay too close for fear of being dashed against it. But we had barely covered a couple of hundred yards when two men and two women burst out of a summer house and rushed down to the shore. "You're the British guys we saw on TV," one of them shouted excitedly. "Come 'n have a beer."

We did not need asking twice.

Chapter Five.
Of Mormons and Mark Twain

One way and another we had now covered about a third of the length of the Mississippi - and in the process overturned many of our pre-conceived ideas of America and the Americans. A lot of mine were rooted in a wartime childhood from which came memories of catch-phrases like "over-paid, over-sexed and over here", and feature films in which quiet, understating, tolerant Brits learned to rub along with glamorous, exuberant and rather naïve Yanks. When my teenage sister brought one home our parents were deeply alarmed, yet I remember him now as a very quiet, very homesick young man who showered me with chewing gum and wrote long, thoughtful letters to his girl's kid sister. I think he was one of the few adults that ever took my 11-year old aspirations seriously.

Probably our more or less common language gives us the illusion that we should be more alike than we appear to be - except that the appearances themselves are based on false assumptions for, with their TV soap operas and banana skin comedies, the Americans can be their own worst publicists. Pre-conditioned I have tended to remember the brash, demanding ones bent on wrenching instant culture from discreet, gracious old Europe. And then there was the US Air Base three miles from our Oxfordshire front door which disturbed my dove-like instincts and regularly shattered our rural calm.

But what of Bill and Louise from Illinois who, on our arrival several years ago, were the first to give us a genuine welcome to the neighbourhood; and a more recent neighbour, Steve, a hawk if ever there was one but who had shown more insatiable interest in our Mississippi plans than many of our indifferent British friends put together?

"You guys really are going?" he said in amazement a week or two before we left, and shook his head in ego-boosting admiration. "I tell you, you gotta be careful. America is a violent country. You don't trust *no one*."

But Steve was from LA and every bit as ignorant of the ways of the Midwest as we had been. So here we were, yet again unquestioningly and with profound gratitude, accepting kindness and generosity thrust upon us by four complete strangers called Joyce and Marion, Marjorie and Paul...

The beers and Cokes turned into a full-scale meal. "Why don't we load you guys and the canoe 'n all on our motor boat and drive you into the city?" was Paul's next suggestion. But George, restored in mind and body, would not hear of it. Instead they took us for a reconnaissance ride to check out the most sheltered route. We roared along at the head of a seething wake, drenched by our own spray, senses battered by wind and engine noise, and it was undeniably exhilarating. Secure, too. Seen from a larger and powered vessel the Mississippi seemed to have preoccupations other than our destruction.

The last stretch under the bridge looked nasty, but at least by the time we got back on the water wind and wave had eased if only a little. We reached the marina beyond the bridge without mishap to find our four friends awaiting us.

The most memorable things about Burlington were the heat and the hospitality. A young journalist on *Hawkeye*, the local paper, gave us a room for a couple of nights in exchange for an interview. We did the sights with Joyce and Marjorie, our mutual enthusiasm rapidly sapped by the heat so that we ended up spending most of the day in leafy shade on the bluffs of Crapo Park, nibbling Kentucky chicken fries and looking down on our river.

It was George's birthday. That evening our friends arranged a barbecue at Joyce and Marion's home, a friendly, untidy, unostentatious house in a suburb. Around midnight Paul took us on a conducted tour of the agricultural machinery plant where he was a foreman.

"Could you imagine a Cowley worker doing the same for an American visitor?" I whispered to George as we passed through silent acres of robots.

"No," George whispered back, "but I *can* imagine an American visitor asking him to."

They all came to see us off at the marina next morning and we settled down to adapt to certain changes that could no longer be ignored. The altered character of the weather was the most drastic. Days of sultry heat were no longer events to be commented upon for every day was as hot and sultry as the last, and we had had a record of seven days without a real storm to temper it. I could understand why the Americans were obsessed with air-conditioning and also knew the humid heat could only get worse.

Out on the river it wasn't quite so bad; but on land every building and the very ground itself absorbed the heat and reflected it back so that we trailed a sauna-like cocoon wherever we went. The former chore of shopping became the highlight of each day with its air-conditioned guarantee, and a bag of ice became a standard item on the shopping list. Tipped into our cooler it would usually see us through 24 hours. I began to understand why Americans were obsessed with ice too.

"At least the river provides its own air-conditioning," George said, and it was true that it could be quite a relief to get back on to it. But the Big Muddy rarely did anything in moderation and for several days the wind blew strong and hard, and right into our faces. When we stopped at Dallas City to seek and obtain permission to camp on their recreation ground we were almost blown back against a quite strong current to the point a mile upstream where we needed to be. It was a bit tricky pitching the tent but the process was enlivened by several visitors, one of them the Mayor's wife waving a newspaper.

70

"Just heard you folks had arrived in town. Saw you in the *Hawkeye*." She thrust that Burlington broadsheet at us and we peered at ourselves smirking out from page one under the heading 'Paddling with pen in hand!'

There was quite a big storm that night but even I didn't complain, grateful for the promise it brought of cooler hours ahead. In any case, though very noisy and very wet I reckoned it registered only about six on my personal Richter scale for Mississippi storms. We spent much of it in Pat's Tap enjoying a convivial evening with a high proportion of the population of Dallas City, which must have been all of 200. A thin young man with a very large girl friend confided they were canoeists too, and returned later to check where we were camping so they could photograph our canoe. Our little waitress was delighted with us and our accents. She kept goats, she told us, and a cow, sheep and some hogs. "And I'm gonna have a baby on Christmas Day, ain't that great?" she said, as confident as though she had placed an order for a Pat's Tap Special; then looked at us doubtfully. "December 25th. S'that the same for you folks over there?"

The character of the river had noticeably changed too. The short stretches of levee which further north had been strategically built to protect communities from the Mississippi's worst excesses now ran for many miles at a time along one or both banks. Likewise the railroads that for so long had flanked our progress now withdrew for long stretches to less vulnerable terrain.

Our close association with them had, in fact, given us a new appreciation of British Rail. The only passenger service to follow the river had been left far behind at La Crosse in Wisconsin. For the rest, the mile-or-more long convoys of battered cargo trucks seemed but a sad echo of the brave new railway age that had caused the demise of the steamboat, and there was a certain irony in comparing them now with the smartly painted tows that had brought commerce back on to the water. All the same we quite missed the mournful hootings of the trains and the creakings and clankings that had punctuated the nights of even our most peaceful camps further north.

Only the Burlington Northern, occasionally switching banks, would remain faithful all the way to St Louis though from time to time other railroads returned briefly to flirt with the riverside, only to vanish again as they headed for some distant part of the continent that did not concern us. Some bore names redolent of long ago.

"Look," I said, perusing the chart. "The Atcheson Topeka and the Santa Fe," and toyed briefly with adolescent memories of the Andrew Sisters and college dances. But George, who had been too busy climbing mountains in those days for such frivolity merely looked uncomprehending.

That particular railroad was carried over our heads by the mighty but disconcertingly low bridge at Fort Madison which, according to our local guide book, was the largest double track swing bridge in the world. As there were not too many trains any more the 'swing' section seemed to be open most of the time to let the tows through and for a nasty moment, with the river running so high, I thought we too would have to cross to the Iowa side to clear it. But a local fisherman assured us we would manage if we kept our heads down, and so it was.

"Next stop Nauvoo," George said. "You'd better practise being good."

I viewed our stay in Nauvoo a little nervously. The name had meant nothing to us until we got down to some preparatory reading for the journey when we learned that it was the historic centre for the Church of Jesus Christ of Latter-Day Saints, more familiar as the Mormons. We were to stay in a private home; I hoped George would restrain himself. Open-minded on most issues he can display marked streaks of agnostic intolerance when confronted with beliefs he considers outrageous. My own belief in a spiritual power for good admits flexibility to accept its interpretation in whatever eccentric form, as long as it is manifestly compassionate and tolerant. With so much, thankfully, still unexplained in this world I do not dare to forecast what is outrageous and what is not in any realm that lies beyond.

"You must admit," George had said when I challenged him, "that stories of inscribed gold plates mysteriously revealed and

72

lost again are a bit hard to take. But of course I'll 'behave myself' as you put it, as a guest in someone's home. At least it'll curb your smoking," he added with a hint of that self-righteousness common to many ex-smokers.

"Not to mention your drinking," I retorted unfairly, for he is a moderate drinker and I was the one who had been obliged to come to terms with an alcohol problem some years earlier.

The Book of Mormon which resulted from the transcription of those gold plates records "God's dealings with the ancient inhabitants of the Americas", how they reached this new promised land from Jerusalem and Babylon in the centuries before Christ, and how in ensuing events of blood and carnage of truly Biblical proportions, they destroyed themselves and each other. Only the Lamanites "principal ancestors of the American Indians" survived, it seems, in a state of moral and spiritual bankruptcy.

According to Mormon belief the plates were sealed and hidden in New York State about 421 AD and it was left until 1823 for them to be miraculously revealed to Joseph Smith, thus after 1400 years restoring to humanity knowledge of the true path to salvation. Joseph and his followers were then guided to spread the glad news, first in Ohio and then in Missouri. But the local inhabitants had other ideas for, in additon to the strangeness of their story, the Mormons' "outrageous beliefs" included an abhorrence of slavery and it was not long before they were run out of several towns. Their wanderings brought them eventually in 1839 to an obscure hamlet on a horseshoe bend of the Mississippi. Joseph Smith called it Nauvoo, adapted from Hebrew meaning "Beautiful Place" and within a few years it was second only to Chicago among Illinois cities, its population over 11,000.

We had been advised to stop at the first grain elevator and announce our arrival by telephone and in due course a truck, a couple of able-bodied men and a pleasant woman called Carmen collected us and our paraphernalia. Carmen and her family were to be our hosts. Their two-storey home stood in a grove of trees and had a reassuring untidiness. When we had cleaned up Carmen made us tea in the kitchen.

"I guess you know we don't drink it, but we don't expect

everyone to follow our ways."

George smiled slightly as he received my signalled message 'Lesson One in tolerance, please note'.

Indeed many of our pre-conceived ideas about the Mormons were given a shake-up that evening. If there was anything unusual about Carmen, her husband Lee, and their happy-go-lucky brood it was their combined serenity and sense of humour. The older children breezed in and out of the house borrowing each other's cars and preparing for a party at which undoubtedly they would neither drink alcohol nor smoke, and seemed uncaring of these forbidden pleasures. As the evening wore on punctuated by telephone calls we observed that Carmen, a trained nurse, seemed to act as unofficial medical adviser and social worker for a steady stream of problems that found their way to her doorstep.

Early on Lee said "Anything you wanna know you only gotta ask." And when we hesitated because some of our questions seemed suddenly impertinent, he went on "Go ahead. We've nothing to hide. Guess you've already seen I'm not concealing any extra wives around the place."

"All right," I said. "What about polygamy?"

Lee grinned. "I guess that's what everyone chooses to remember us best for. Yeah, polygamy was allowed once, even encouraged by our early prophets because of the shortage of men in our following. But that was a long time ago and never really practised by the RLDS." We looked puzzled. "The Reorganized Church of Latter Day Saints."

Ah yes the church, like many another before it, had split over the interpretation of its scriptures. In their fine city with its grid plan, brick buildings and magnificent temple under construction, the troubled inhabitants had been rent by dissension from within and fear and suspicion from without. Joseph Smith had been jailed at nearby Carthage and murdered by an angry mob, violent with alarm and incomprehension, in 1844. Two years later Brigham Young had led most of the rest of his persecuted flock across an unusually frozen Mississippi to begin the arduous search for a new Jerusalem which ended in Salt Lake City. The RLDS had later re-formed and made its headquarters in Independence, Missouri. Both branches now worked for the rebuilding of Nauvoo, and antipathy had been replaced to a large degree by mutual tolerance though each firmly pursued its own doctrines - and maintained its own visitors' centre.

Much of Nauvoo is now a pleasant park in which old buildings are being restored and destroyed ones rebuilt according to original plans; among them next day we saw the homes of Joseph Smith and Brigham Young, and a scale model that echoed the lavishness of the temple destroyed by an unknown arsonist two years after the exodus. Outside the modern LDS Visitors Centre there was a gentle statue of Joseph Smith and his wife, Emma. Inside immensely courteous and well groomed young men greeted us and offered to answer our questions. From time to time we had had mirror images of them on our doorstep in Oxfordshire.

The Mormon Church is said to be the fastest growing in the Christian world. Our guide that day had become a convert over twenty years earlier. Over lunch we tackled him gently over the plausibility of the gold plates but he merely said "Many stranger things have happened," and this was difficult to refute.

Barely had the Mormons departed from Nauvoo when there was another strange influx, this time dedicated to perhaps America's first and only experiment in Communism. Most of its followers originated in France. Their mission was to create a Utopian community based on their leader Etienne Cabet's book 'Voyage en Icarie'. We had not heard of it, but it explained why they called themselves the Icarians.

So, the Mormons' abandoned homes were taken over, the remaining stones of their destroyed temple used to build others, and the Icarians set about establishing a community based on true brotherhood, peace, justice and fair shares for all. Alas it survived only a few years, but from it Nauvoo inherited some more charming buildings and a thriving wine industry whose repertoire still featured, according to George, a very acceptable Burgundy.

He made this pronouncement, the sole imbiber, as we dined at the Nauvoo Hotel on our last evening with Carmen, Lee and two of their daughters. The hotel, described as being built in early Mormon style, dated from the 1840s and was very attractive. Restoration had included the use of bricks from Joseph Smith's general store. What, I wondered, as we passed the cocktail lounge, would he have thought of that?

Soon after Nauvoo we successfully negotiated the largest of all the Mississippi's locks at Keokuk and after 20 uneventful miles found with some difficulty a corner of maize field in which to camp. It never ceased to surprise us how ill-informed many people were about the river, even those who lived right by her. Time and again we were directed to 'wild' or official camp sites that lay drowned under inches or even feet of water, and more than once were obliged to scramble up steep, muddy banks, involving a great deal of laborious hauling through tangled undergrowth in order to find a few dry square feet for the night.

But the river policeman at hot, sleepy Canton, Missouri, a couple of days after Nauvoo really should have known better. We had landed to do some shopping and in the process set foot for the first time in our fifth State. "No problem," the policeman said. "Cross over to the Illinois side and take Canton Chute. About eight miles down you'll find a real good camp site."

"What about the high water?" I asked.

"No problem," he said again. "Level's bin droppin' several days now."

"Not so as you'd notice," I muttered as we headed for Canton Chute. "No problem, no problem - how often have we heard that just before some disaster?"

But I was glad we would be out of the navigation channel and in what looked like sheltered waters for most of the way. The river was beginning to get at me again. The continuous heat did not help and ironically the stiff headwind that now tempered it made progress not only hard won but exceedingly slow.

Inside my head arguments were beginning to take shape. We had reached the fifth out of ten States and paddled just about 500 miles. In a few days, Mississippi-willing, we would reach St Louis, the first major city since we left Minneapolis.

St Louis I had always considered rather inaccurately to be about our half way mark. Surely it would not be so very defeatist to throw in the towel then? Everyone else was so darned keen to follow our shining example it wouldn't, couldn't be difficult to find an eager volunteer to take my place in the canoe. I would rent a car and act as support party, buying all the food, setting up camps. The idea became increasingly desirable and sane, and I had just decided to await the right moment - that evening perhaps once we were comfortably installed in camp - to present it to George when he said "Bloody water skiers."

We had forgotten it was Saturday. Canton Chute was alive with the weekend brigade, roaring and swishing and "hulloo-ing" with a carefree indulgence that only emphasised our own tedious efforts. We kept close to the shore, creeping past the row of riverside summer houses perched up on their stilts, and past their jetties from which our tormentors came and went. The eight miles turned out to be nearer twelve during which I finally managed to switch on to automatic, both mentally and physically. We left the resort area behind and at last in the distance ahead made out a clearing in the trees, and objects that might be picnic tables. And then we arrived.

"Oh Lord," said George in a tone that summed it all up.

We beached the canoe and squelched our way from one end of the site to the other. The river had indeed dropped, but only just. The place was a mess. Eventually we found a flattish, dryish patch close to the two loos on their traditional perch on a small mound.

"At least," I said brightly, "there'll be no problem getting the pegs in." While George unloaded I pitched the tent. We surveyed the sadly sagging result.

"Looks like how I feel," George said, and for some reason the sight of our despondent tent cheered us both up. Stripping off we wallowed at the river's edge, savouring the brief illusion of coolness; but as the wind dropped the whole world seemed to hold its breath in a suffocating stillness. Neither of us could eat much and, when darkness brought the first mosqui-toes, we crawled into the tent to lie saturated in sweat and listen to the first distant tremor of a storm.

I must have slept for I came to abruptly as George hurriedly closed the zip of the flysheet seconds before a blinding blue flash coincided with a mind-splitting salvo and a torrent of water hit the tent.

Even the worst of our earlier storms had worked up to a crescendo; this one began on a crescendo and stayed there, seemingly poised immediately above the tent. I remember once having foolishly let myself be persuaded to attend a 'Cosmic Laser Concert' in Canada and stumbling out of the auditorium seconds after it began, my mind frantic to escape. Here was nature's equivalent and there was no escape. It was like Armageddon in Sound and Light, and the fear it brought was a raw animal terror as I clung to George as though life itself depended on it. It was not reasonable for rational thought to survive such an assault on the senses. And yet...

An unfamiliar sensation penetrated fear and touched a residue of reason. There was something odd about my elbow, or rather the squashy softness on which it leant. I probed about. The softness was everywhere.

"I think we're afloat," I bawled at George, and with action now urgent a flicker of sanity returned.

We were out of the tent like squibs. Unable to cope with the volume of water inflicted on it from above the soggy camp site was rapidly transforming into a rising tide of mud.

"Women's loo," yelled George.

We grabbed armfuls of our saturated belongings and stumbled, slid, fell, picked ourselves up and stumbled on, back and forth, until everything that was remotely portable was stacked in an unholy heap of mud and disorder in the confines of the tiny shed. From its doorway we looked out on the desolation of ebony dark and glinting water that quivered in the intermittent glare and unrelenting roar.

But no longer quite so unrelenting. "What about the tent?" I asked wearily and found I didn't have to shout any more.

"It'll be OK now," George said, for we could actually count the seconds between lightning and thunder and the torrent had become recognisable as rain. "But let's get the canoe tied up."

Between us hung the unspoken thought that the storm would

probably return.

Back in the loo there were two lavatory seats, without doors but separated by a partition. We sat on them and surveyed the mess. It was 2.15 a.m. Only a short time earlier we had been devastated by the heat; now I shivered uncontrollably. A bit of rummaging yielded a dry sweater apiece. George made a brave effort to produce some coffee, but water had got into both stoves. We lit a candle and sat swatting at mosquitoes that had come to share the refuge with us, the rain reduced now to a steady tattoo.

"In all my vast experience," George said, "I've never chalked up a night in a women's loo before," and for some reason it touched a nerve and I burst into tears.

At last I said, "I can't go on, you know. I really can't. There are times when this river makes me mindless. I hate it so, this being afraid, and feeling inadequate, and pretending everything's all right. I *know* there have been a lot of good times, but nothing, absolutely nothing, is worth this feeling of total mindless fear. You don't know what it's like to be really afraid."

It wasn't true, I knew. You could not be shot down, a prisoner-of-war for three years, the sole survivor of an avalanche, face nature at its rawest and most uncompromising as he had done many times and never be afraid. But mine was far more a fear of losing grip on sanity; it had nearly happened once and I never wanted to touch that nightmare world again.

George let me ramble on as I spilled out the plan so rationally worked out a few hours earlier. For once he did not try to reassure or change my mind, only saying when at last I dried up, "We'll talk about it when we're out of this mess."

I sat on a loo seat propped up by a rucksack, too emotionally flattened to react when the storm returned. Eons later, but quite suddenly as though someone had flicked a celestial switch, all became quiet again except for water dripping from the trees and a murmur from the river. The faintest lightening of the darkness brought a filter of grey seeping through cracks in the door. And then a bird sang.

"I don't believe it," I said, as the soft hesitant chirrup developed into rich, confident song, and was taken up by another, and another.

79

In a few moments the dawn chorus was at full throttle and we stood outside our tiny refuge looking out upon a sodden world that was otherwise almost unbelievable in its normality.

It was 5 a.m. We bundled our disordered belongings into the canoe and set off the four miles to the next town, Quincy. The river was at her most exquisite, her placid waters barely ruffled by the faintest breeze, the veils of mist shifting and dissolving in the first shafts of the sun.

"You lousy hypocrite," I muttered. "You don't fool me."

At Quincy we left the cannoe in a marina near a large river boat from which emanated a discordant assortment of tuning-up sounds. It bore a banner announcing 'American Symphony Wind Orchestra' and we later learned it was a floating concert hall for a youth orchestra from Philadelphia. Just then, though, I was only interested in more prosaic matters like breakfast, a bath and, above all, a bed.

A policeman told us about a camp site a mile up river but this time I was firm. We booked into the Quincy Motor Inn and within an hour, with the help of the hotel truck, had transferred the bulk of our soggy belongings into a dishevelled pile on the balcony outside our room. We soaked the tent and mattresses in the bath and draped them over the balcony rail to dry. Unasked a cleaning lady marched in with a pile of towels. "Guess you could use these," she said.

It was a day of washing and drying and brushing and scraping, punctuated by blissful interludes of sleep and a foray to a laundromat. I savoured every humdrum detail. By the end of it our equipment at least was in good order again except for the stoves, both of which defied George's attempts to repair them.

"Let's hope we can get them fixed in Hannibal," he said, giving up at last in exasperation. Fortunately it was only a day's paddle to that heartland of Tom Sawyer and Huckleberry Finn where we planned a two-night stay.

Nothing more had been said about my plans to abandon the expedition. I knew George's enviable capacity to believe that if you ignore certain problems they will simply go away, and there was no point in harping on it at the moment. With the benefit of several hours sleep and a day of normality the decision had lost some of its urgency, but I had absolutely no intention of letting this particular problem simply go away. In that respect we are very different. George thrives on challenges, actively seeking them out when they don't happen to come along of their own accord. Conversely I have found that while the overcoming of obstacles is necessary and desirable, one of the biggest of life's challenges is accepting your own limitations. It is not always easy to distinguish between pride and courage.

The immediate problem was whether this was a case in point. I almost hoped we would have a difficult journey to Hannibal to help restore the resolve which had seemed so unassailable during the awful night of the storm.

We did not. The Mississippi was at her most beguiling. A gentle steady current carried us with almost no effort on our part. Tempered by the storm the temperature stuck pleasantly in the lower 80s° F. The faintest breeze was at our backs and on it drifted the fluffy white cottonwood seeds that settled like snow flakes on water as still as glass. Despite a late start we had covered the 19 miles to Hannibal by 2 p.m. As we moored in the marina a replica sternwheeler chugged away on a sightseeing cruise with a cheery toot. There were no prizes for guessing her name, the *Mark Twain*.

Samuel was little more than a toddler when the Clemens family moved to Hannibal in the 1830s, and he was still in his teens when he moved out into the big world beyond. But with him he took the memories of a childhood and a way of life that would enchant future generations of every age and many nations as he relived them in the adventures of *Tom Sawyer* and *Huckleberry Finn*.

Long before that, though, Sam became a qualified riverboat pilot. His account of that period in *Life on the Mississippi* is a verbal monument to the river and to riverboat pilots. I have read no more vivid or intimate account of the Big Muddy in its every mood, nor of the stupefying feats of memory of the pilots themselves. Every homestead, tree and bush along every inch of her banks; every snag in or under her waters;

every shoal, headland, cove and islet, had to be imprinted on the mind and then, with infallible accuracy, related to depths that could change by the hour and non-visibility of a pitch black night or swirling fog. Men with such minds hardly seem mortal. It was the river, too, that gave Sam Clemens his pen name, 'Mark Twain' being one of the oft-repeated cries of the leadsmen announcing the river depth - in this case two fathoms.

Hannibal has squeezed the last drop of capital from its gratuitous asset as his childhood home. There is a Tom'n Huck Hotel, a Huck Finn Shopping Centre, a Becky Thatcher bookshop, Aunt Polly Handcrafts and a dozen other premises perpetuating the characters of his fictional world. More serious students find all they need in the Visitors' Centre on Hill Street adjoining Sam Clemens' boyhood home. Of white clapboard and green shutters, its garden is bright with roses and petunias behind the famous long white fence that featured in the Tom Sawyer story. But amongst the memorabilia and the documents there are more sombre hints of the solitary man who came to despair of much in his America.

Nearly thirty years after his departure Samuel Clemens returned to Hannibal on a nostalgic visit and found "The people... are not more changed than is the town. It is no longer a village; it is a city, with a mayor, and a council, and water works, and probably a debt.... The customary half-dozen railways center in Hannibal now... In my time the town had no specialty, and no commercial grandeur; the daily packet usually landed a passenger and bought a catfish, and took away another passenger and a hatful of freight; but now a huge commerce in lumber has grown up and a large miscellaneous commerce is one of the results..."

Among other results were certain amenities that would have quite horrified the respectable citizenry of his boyhood days. Bag and baggage we headed now for one of them in aptly named Bird Street and just before a towering grain elevator on the waterfront turned into No. 111 under a sign. 'Bed and Breakfast', it said in small letters under the much larger brazen ones that spelt 'BORDELLO'.

82

Chapter Six
"Meet me in St Louis"

"Do you Dare Tell The Folks Back Home Where You Stayed In Hannibal?!!!" asked The Bordello's bright pink brochure.

"I don't think I'd dare tell the folks Back in Nauvoo," I said to George as we dumped our rucksacks upstairs in Room No. 3. There were seven rooms altogether opening out on to the wide central corridor.

Richard, who had acquired the establishment for more orthodox tourist purposes, gave us a conducted tour. He was a tall thin young man with a goatee beard and wiry energy.

"The girls didn't live in - only worked here you understand," he explained as we popped in and out of rooms that were neat and clean but quite sparsely furnished. Presumably if business were brisk no one had been encouraged to feel too much at home.

Downstairs the restaurant was dominated by a huge mural depicting some of The Girls hanging out of an upstairs window of No. 111 gesticulating at passing vessels. They looked more jolly than seductive to me but I probably was not the best judge. Richard presented me with a Bordello T-shirt which caused some sniggers next day when I wore it for a jaunt on the Twinland Express, a bright yellow road train that trundled us on a 12-mile circuit in and around Hannibal. We ended up that evening at Mark Twain Reflections, a rather good amateur open-air enactment of events, mainly from *Tom Sawyer*. After the show the characters mingled with the audience and little girls became starry-eyed with the attentions of Tom Sawyer and Huck Finn.

We rounded off the evening in The Bordello's restaurant. Richard introduced us to a smart fellow in early middle age called Jay, who looked as though he might be in real estate or insurance and turned out to own companies in both.

"You guys are gonna have a drink with with me," he announced. "And when you get to Louisiana you're gonna be my guests. It's the greatest little town on the river, and Martha and me would just love to show you around."

Until then I had not noticed that, as well as a Louisiana State at the end of our journey, there was a Louisiana town just a day's paddling downstream. Any prospect of a bed with its guarantee of air-conditioning and immunity from direct exposure to heat, gale or storm was extremely attractive. George was grateful but non-commital. The future of the expedition had not been discussed further and, for the moment at least, I had postponed any final decision until St Louis.

The river continued to behave impeccably. With nothing more distressing than a steady flurry of cottonwood seeds to tickle our noses, I found time to study the map as the current and an amenable breeze wafted us in the general direction of the Gulf of Mexico.

The growing list of riverside communities that we had left behind represented nothing less than a random hop, skip and jump round the Old World. It seemed a lifetime since way up in north-west Minnesota we had begun our journey in Latin at Lake Itasca. Since then we had ricocheted through at least half a dozen European countries, with occasional forays into North Africa and the Middle East and a few contributions from the native Indians. Yet out of all those waves of settlers and the new immigrants that had imposed upon them the ways of Ireland or Germany, Scandinavia or Middle Europe, the Balkans or the Levant - out of all that melée there had been distilled something that could only be American, and

Midwest American at that.

We reached Louisiana quite comfortably by late afternoon to be hailed by voices from a ramshackle shed on stilts. It was the Louisiana Boat Clubhouse. Everyone knew Jay.

"Sure he meant it," they said when we expressed doubts about pursuing the invitation. "He'll be real mad if you don't call him. Phone's over there."

And within minutes we were being whirled round the little town at the receiving end of a barrage of local information. "You're gonna love this place. I guess you'll wanna see the plastics plant ...yeah, and the cardboard cylinder factory. I'll fix that up for tomorrow. Over there is my office by the way, and across the road that's the old folks' home I built. Guess you know about our apples? The Stark Nurseries? Red and Golden Delicious? Right here, that's where they come from ...cuttings sent out all over the world." And there was a lot more. Something on the car dashboard started squealing urgently. Jay flicked a switch. "Fuzz-buster - tells me when the cops are around. Kinda useful." He grinned. "Great guys. Know 'em all anyway. Guess we'd better head for home. Martha's so excited about your visit."

Met in the Champs Elysées or the Piazza San Marco, Jay might have been a bit hard going but in Louisiana, Missouri, he was an admirable host. His home, a gracious two-storeyed brick building approached up a long winding drive through a landscaped park, undeniably had style. Martha was a neat pretty woman, as serene as her husband was not.

"You guys'll wanna bath," he said as soon as introductions were over, and we now accepted that conversation with Jay consisted largely of a series of statements or purely rhetorical questions. So we obediently had a bath, just as obediently followed by a drink and then a tour of the grounds to see the man-made lake that was lit up at night, and the imported "Royal" mute swans that glided over the reflections of the specially planted hickory trees.

Jay was in charge of the meal. There was corn on the cob, barbecued steak, baked potatoes and salad. "You'll never wanna eat anything else," he announced happily as the corn began to sizzle in butter. And later "You'll never taste steak like

85

this again." And it was all admittedly very good.

Afterwards over coffee in the big comfortable living room he pointed to a wall. "See those bricks - bought 'em from the first schoolhouse where I was educated, and the beams, they're from Martha's folks' barn. Over there, that's a real Victorian clock of Mom's. And the stained glass lamp - my daughter made that. Now she's a real artist..."

Listening to him I suddenly saw that behind all the self-assurance the reality of Jay's life had been built like the house, brick by brick, every event and relationship dependent on the reassurance of some tangible treasure. What, I wondered, would happen if for some reason a brick fell out of place? Then I observed Martha watching him with her serene smile and knew what the answer would be.

Fortunately, for one reason or another Jay was not able to arrange any visits to plastics or cardboard cylinder factories next morning. But he did put a call through to Clarksville to tell them we were on the way. This little community's claim to fame was its Sky Ride to "the highest peak on the Mississippi River between St Paul and New Orleans."

"You'll never see another view like it," Jay had told us. "Eight hundred square miles of God's own country."

We found quite a few of them shrouded in a heat haze when the Sky Ride's chairlift deposited us on the summit at 600 feet, but it was undeniably a rare view and, more particularly, it virtually overhung Lock 24. A tow with a convoy of 15 barges slid toy-like over the broad ribbon of the river that shimmered like crumpled tinfoil. Through binoculars we watched the whole locking through process unfold as on an aerial film. When we got down to the riverside again there seemed an unusual number of people hanging about the lock.

"Yeah," the lockmaster confirmed. "The *Delta Queen*'ll be through in an hour."

So we had our first encounter with that legendary doyen of the Mississippi, the last of the genuine sternwheelers plying the river and America's only floating registered historical monument. We had seen plenty of old prints of major river ports, their quays lined with such vessels - sidewheelers and sternwheelers

- two or three deep, smoke belching from their high stacks. The competition for trade between their owners had been fearsome, especially in the steamboating heyday that followed the Civil War when they beat up and down the river in their thousands.

Sometimes captains would take on side bets for a race and, with engines straining and sparks flying, the spectacle drew cheering supporters at every riverside town. Astonishingly the record set by the *Robert E Lee* in her race against the *Natchez* in 1870 still stands: 3 days, 13 hours and 14 minutes to cover the thousand-plus miles from New Orleans to St Louis - against the current.

In their efforts to improve their schedules many steamboats paid the ultimate price - and often their crews and passengers with them. Overworked boilers blew up, snags and sand bars took their toll, a careless spark in a bale of straw or cotton could fire an uncontrollable blaze. The average life of a steamboat was 18 months. Down on the river bed as the silt piled up round rotting timbers, many a vessel became the embryo for yet another sand bar to catch the unwary.

But the *Delta Queen*, now a cosseted monument turned floating luxury hotel for an elite of tired millionaires, had survived since her Glasgow-built hull first slid into the water in 1926. It was disappointing to learn she had been built in California not by the Mississippi, but she looked magnificent as she eased gently into Lock 24 and departed again, her sternwheel churning up a trailing chaos of water.

"Best not meet her without plenty of room to spare," George said, more prophetically than he certainly intended.

Further subtle changes in the character of the river were emerging. Shore-side communities were now becoming increasingly further apart; in the 70 miles between Clarksville and Alton there were no more than three tiny places, plus a handful of resort areas which did not merit mention on the charts unless they had a marina. Riverside roads were rare; instead dirt tracks linked perhaps a score of access points with the highway system that had mostly retreated several miles. After our little spate of Midwest towns the river had once more reverted for long stretches to a wilderness solitude; more lush,

87

though, than earlier for now trailing green curtains of creeper and vine added their confirmation that we had entered a different climatic zone.

And at last the level of the water was noticeably dropping. At a lone marina the owner was doing some running repairs to his landing stage.

"Twenny five years I've worked by this river and there ain't bin a summer like this one," he said, shaking his head ruefully. "Spring floods, okay. But high water like this in summer? Three, four times, we've cleaned up, bin flooded out, cleaned up agin. It's bin a tough year."

He came and sat with us while we sucked at cans of beer and 7-Up, and commiserated over the behaviour of some of his customers.

"Some of them cowboys oughta be run off the river. See that?" He pointed to the 'No Wash' sign indicating that engines should be throttled back on approaching the landing stage. "You should see 'em roaring up full speed, and the mayhem it causes. Sucks in the river banks, destroys my piers, makes a lotta trouble for the folks jist out enjoyin' themselves. Weekend warriors we call 'em. Full of how important they think they are, and usually full of beer, too." He shook his head again. "Things ain't what they used to be."

We asked him about sand bars for camping, and he said "Sure they're comin' up out of the river fast now. It's a real shame she's bin so high else you'd have found 'em all along - beautiful, real beautiful." He flicked over the page of the chart we'd brought up from the canoe and jabbed it with a stubby finger. "That's a real beaut in about seven miles; guess you'll be lookin' for a good place 'bout then."

He wandered down to the canoe with us and sent us off with a final warning. "When you get to the pool above Alton, watch out. I tell you down there them weekend warriors are fightin' over every square inch of them sand bars. If anyone gives you guys any trouble, you write down their number and tell the river cops. Take care now."

This time we had not been misled. Within a very few miles we started seeing sand bars and whether or not we selected our marina friend's 'real beaut' our choice was fine by us.

Now at last we learned what we had been missing all these past weeks for a Mississippi sand bar has all the attributes desirable for the ideal canoe-camp site. Firstly the canoe could be slid out of the water with the greatest ease. Secondly it could be unloaded free of the earlier encumbrances of tree roots, tangled undergrowth and all-invasive mud. Thirdly now armed with sand pegs tent pitching was simplicity itself. Finally with no access by road and the water too shallow for any weekend warrior, our privacy was guaranteed.

We followed our usual practice of unloading, pitching the tent, brewing coffee, setting up the kitchen and sleeping quarters, and then went for a walk. In this respect the sand bar was a bit limited for when we reached the top of a nearby hummock fringed with bushes and trees we found we were on an island separated by a narrow strait from the Illinois shore. But there were plenty of other distractions, like the contorted shapes of driftwood stranded by the receding waters, and the network of animal spoor and bird prints, evidence that our particular scrap of Robinson Crusoeland by no means lacked other invaders.

It was all that a camp site should be right down to the spectacular sunset that burnished gold streaks into the river and sent the sky flaring over the Missouri shore. Even the mosquitoes were less than usually troublesome so that late in the evening we re-emerged from the tent to wander along the edge of the river, now silver and black, the sand already cool under our feet, the stars thick overhead and the winking green light of a starboard marker over on the Missouri shore. We were only a hundred yards or so from the navigation channel. Twice during the night a tow thrummed quietly by. A searchlight flickered briefly over the tent and I stuck my head out to watch the black bulk of the convoy slip by. For minutes afterwards its wash hissed rhythmically against the sand a few yards away and for much longer the hum of the tow's engine hung on the air. Then stillness - and, yes, an awareness of the strangest sensation that came close to affection for the Big Muddy.

The feeling endured all of 12 hours until Lock 25.

Since the near-fiasco just before the Quad Cities the locks had given us an easy time. There had been the occasional wait if a tow preceded us or one was locking through from downstream; in such cases we would retreat into a backwater or, in the absence of this, land a few hundred yards upstream to wait until the red signal turned to amber. It still amazed us each time the huge machinery slid into action in the sole interest of our tiny craft and, even more so, when a great convoy of barges was actually held back in recognition of our prior claim. For a long run of locks now it had all worked like a charm and my earlier apprehension of them had gradually become, if not eliminated, at least lulled.

Now there were only three more locks to go and I suppose we were overdue for a hiccup.

Everything seemed normal enough on the approach to Lock 25. A tow was preparing to go through and, with the sluice gates open and the current brisk, we sheltered in a small backwater behind a wing dam some distance upstream of the lock entrance. A small inflatable was chugging about in little circles waiting too.

"We'll have to paddle *hard* when it's our turn," George warned. Of course it took us much longer than motorised folk to get into the lock and we were always very conscious of the delay we inevitably caused. With the river so active I was not at all keen that we should leave our sheltered corner too soon. But the wing dam blocked our view of the control signals so we nosed out cautiously from time to time to check the situation and teeter on the fringe of the current like nervous old ladies at the edge of the sea.

At last the tow disappeared, the lock gates re-opened and, as the inflatable moved forward, George said "Right, let's go."

We paddled furiously but even with the helpful current we didn't make it; nor, despite its engine, did the inflatable. While we were still some distance away the lock gates closed firmly in our faces. It had never happened before. By the time we reached the guide wall the inflatable's crew were furiously pulling the signal cord, and we all made angry noises while our two craft bobbed up and down in impotent indignation. There was a long pause while nothing seemed to happen and then, rising imperiously above the lock gates, a superstructure that was quite unmistakeable came into view.

"Damnation," George said. It was the *Delta Queen*.

"Let's get out of here," I said, trying not to whimper but with vivid memories of the *Queen's* sternwheel in action as she emerged from Lock 24. Against such a current it was easier said than done and it took exceeding effort to inch our way back into the calm beyond the wing dam.

The inflatable retreated ahead of us. One of its occupants called over "Take it easy folks. We'll tell those guys to hold it for you next time." We waved a grateful acknowledgment and once again teetered anxiously trying to gauge the right moment. As the lock gates opened yet again we were not really in the mood to appreciate the magnificent sight of the *Delta Queen* at close quarters, nor the amazed expressions of some of her passengers. The turbulence was fearsome but the We-no-nah, bucking and rolling, weathered it bravely as we flailed our way towards the lock.

And to no avail. As the inflatable entered the lock chamber ahead of us, the gates inexorably closed in our faces again.

Too incensed to be frightened any more I hung on the bell cord. After a long pause the gates opened for a third time, just wide enough to disgorge a lone motor boat; and for a third time they began to close. But on this occasion our combined lung power took effect for a surprised face appeared and vanished, and the half closed gates re-opened.

An unusual number of spectators, presumably drawn by the passage of the *Delta Queen*, crowded the rails.

"Get me the lockmaster," yelled George at them, too angry to remember the niceties, and almost immediately a worried and apologetic face appeared overhead. The lockmaster was off duty; he was the deputy. He was real sorry for giving us a rough time. He might well look worried too for we now saw that the forward barges of a large tow were jammed almost against the far side of the downstream gates leaving only the narrowest passage once they opened. Time and again we had been warned against getting close to a tow, even when stationary, especially the forward end and especially when there was a current running; the undertow could be fiendish.

"Three times," George was exploding. "Three times you've shut those bloody gates in our faces. We've had nothing but courtesy and efficiency at every other lock on the river. " I could see he was getting into his stride. "And this is an absolute disgrace." He waved an arm at the waiting tow. "And what are you going to do about *that?*"

"Yeah, sure, sure, I'll tell the cap'n to back off." The face retreated hurriedly.

"And remember you're responsible for our safety," George shouted after it, adding more quietly "Better put life jackets on."

I didn't need telling twice. The convoy backed off but not much and there was still precious little space to creep by, with the water fanning out through the sluice gates on our port side as we emerged and the massive overhanging wall of the convoy's forward end only feet away to starboard. The We-no-nah faltered but only momentarily, then we were swept alongside the barges, all quarter-mile of them, and at last out on to the open river.

The episode had lasted over two hours and the previous night's love affair with the Mississippi was forgotten as I scoured the banks for a place where we could get off her as rapidly as possible. A marina was marked on the chart but somehow we missed it and there followed nine miles of increasingly hot and wearisome paddling along a shoreline whose tangled growth offered no easy escape. It was also, yet again, a Saturday and the pleasure traffic building up as we drew closer to a resort area. Soon we were in the thick of it.

Like so many hornets motor boats of every size buzzed and hummed and roared. A barge convoy chugged upstream. Water skiers and their tow were riding its wash and other motor boats crossing in front of it with what seemed to us an insane disregard for life and limb. The river, quite calm only a mile back, now seethed crossly with the combined activity of scores of boats that seemed to be going nowhere in particular but made our progress exceedingly uncomfortable and, at times, alarming. With the traumas of Lock 25 and 24 miles of paddling behind us since our idyllic sand bar, it was beginning to seem a very long day.

The several marinas were all crowded and unappealing. From one of them we were directed to Kinders Restaurant, a couple of miles down river on the Illinois shore. When we got there after a rocky and wretched journey the landing stages and terraces were packed respectively with boats and humanity. As a camp site it looked very unpromising.

Feeling unkempt and totally out of tune with the prevailing holiday mood we were trailing up to the restaurant when someone caught my arm. "Say, are you guys really Britishers?" I turned to see a stocky man with a friendly face. "Hi," he said, "I saw you paddling in with your Union Jack. I'm Jim Williams and I know just the place for you tonight."

He had a friend called Dusty with him. Moments later we were having a drink and very willingly letting our lives be taken over again. Jim was an airline pilot and also the owner of a sleek white motor cruiser moored down at the landing stage. It was equipped with a radio phone and he lived a dozen miles away. Almost before we knew we had agreed his wife Suzi had been told to expect guests for the night and arrangements made with the restaurant to take care of our canoe and equipment. Soon we were roaring back up river to the marina we had just left in a vessel we might well have roundly cursed in other circumstances. A short car ride later we arrived in an elegant residential area.

Suzi was very young and extremely pretty, and the house was one of the most impeccably manicured I have seen outside the pages of a glossy magazine. I would have laid a bet on the next suggestion.

"Guess you could use a bath," Jim said and left us gazing upon an enormous pink oval sunken bath set below a wall-sized mirror in which our dishevelled reflections looked extremely out of place.

When we emerged Jim was organising a barbecue and pouring drinks. He told us that when he wasn't flying planes he dabbled in pop music recordings.

"That's where I started off, in show business. Would you believe I was on the same bill sometimes as Elvis Presley? A long time ago." He grinned. "The kids were busy chucking bottles at me at the same time they were throwing bouquets

93

at him. So I got the message. But he was a helluva nice guy Elvis in those days. Unassuming, generous, kind."

"Can't say I like the noise he made," George said with unusual understatement.

It was a restful evening during which Jim asked a lot about our journey and finally said "I'm real glad we met. Guess I wish I'd got the guts to do what you're doing."

I felt a terrible fraud. "I'm running scared a lot of the time."

"Takes more guts when you're scared," Jim said.

He and George talked flying. Jim was on domestic runs just then "So it's great being so near the airport. I can be home with Suzi most evenings."

I asked which airport and Jim looked surprised. "St Louis. From here it's only 15 miles to down town."

It was a revelation. My vision of geography so long constricted by the river and our creeping progress down it was suddenly confronted by the smallness of the commuter's world. Fifty river miles and a couple of days were summarily reduced to a few minutes spin along a turnpike. I burst out laughing at the absurdity of it.

Nevertheless 50 river miles it remained as far as we were concerned. Jim, Suzi and their precocious three-year-old son came to see us off next day and hovered nearby in their smart white boat for a couple of miles while Jim took photographs of us at every angle. Then "We'll go find a sand bar now. Give us a call when you get to St Louis," he shouted and in seconds was reduced to a tiny speck above a trail of foam.

It was another day of little wind and merciless heat and as we got closer to the pool above Alton the current lost all significance. Scenically it was an interesting section for the bluffs had returned, real cliffs of sheer limestone almost to the river's edge in the last miles. In one major respect, too, we had cause to be grateful for in the wide pool above the town the weekend hordes were reduced to distant dots well over towards the Missouri shore. We clung thankfully to the Illinois side, able to concentrate on the mechanical dip and draw of our paddles, and wiping the sweat from our eyes. George was suffering badly from dehydration and after a brief stop at a tavern we lay up for an hour or two in the shade of a tree. But it only seemed hotter than ever when we go back on the river and we reached Alton with huge relief.

Harry Button was our contact there and he came to pick us up from a marina just north of town, armed with a batch of leaflets. From these we learned that Alton had made its mark on history as the venue for a major debate on the slavery issue between Abraham Lincoln and Stephen Douglas in 1858. It had also fathered the tallest man in the world. By all accounts a gentle giant the poor fellow had reached 6 ft. 2½ ins by the age of eight and died at 22 in 1940, topping 8 ft. 11 ins.

There were some pleasant old houses in the down town area below and on the bluffs but the town was predominantly industrial, its waterfront dominated by a huge grain elevator. In river terms we had our reasons for wanting to meet the master of Alton's Lock 26 and Harry fixed this up next day. Apart from being the last but one of all the Mississippi's locks it was also the first to handle the double weight of traffic from both the Mississippi and Illinois rivers, all the way from distant Chicago and the Great Lakes-St Lawrence Seaway. We had slipped across the Illinois' surprisingly modest mouth a few miles upstream.

"That's right," Tom Durham confirmed as we chatted in his office up above the lock chamber. "About 60% of my traffic comes from the Illinois and this lock's bin handling almost double what it was built for. We've had to devise all kinda ploys to keep the traffic movin' and even then when it's real busy some of them cap'ns have to wait, can be 48 hours." We noted thankfully there was an auxiliary lock for smaller barges and the likes of us. But help was at hand for Tom, for a couple of miles downstream a massive new lock and dam system nearing completion would be able to handle a full tow in one lockage, halving the time.

Winter brought different problems he told us. The Illinois river was kept open year round all the way to Chicago, while in normal winters the Mississippi was negotiable as far as Keokuk. But like its summers, Mississippi winters could be far from normal.

"In a bad season," Tom said, "the tows can get locked in the ice for weeks at a time. As the pressure builds up they're shoved every which way across the river. And they still have to be manned and provisioned. Happens they have to fly in provisions by helicopter; relief crews too." It was hard even to think of ice with day time temperatures now rarely below the 90°s F, but Tom showed us photographs of white landscapes on which scattered convoys looked like abandoned toys. "When the water starts flowin' through the open sluices to loosen 'em up, that's somethin' to see."

Only 26 miles separated us now from the heart of St Louis. A few miles downstream the even mightier waters of the Missouri joined the Mississippi and the two jostled along in uneasy partnership around the sweep of a great bend. It was said to be a treacherous stretch of water over a rocky bed and we had every intention of avoiding it by following the alternative route: the 10-mile cut of the Chain of Rocks canal.

With two locks to negotiate and no current at all on the canal section it was a long way in one day, especially as we needed to arrive in the city as early as possible. All round, an interim camp was desirable. But where in this increasingly industrialised landscape?

Harry Button found the answer: an irregular green patch on the chart marked "Lewis and Clark State Memorial Park". "Better check it out," he said reaching for the phone, "else you'll have the cops moseying around."

It was a rough ride for a few miles the next day after an easy passage through Lock 26 and a cheery wave from its master. The combination of construction work on the new lock and dam and a continuous series of busy barge terminals and shipyards had us scuttling like frightened mice in and out between moored convoys, trying to keep out of the way of manoeuvring vessels even as we bounced vigorously in their wash. But it was a short paddling day and we came very soon to the State Memorial Park set in the angle between the Mississippi and a narrow creek. Directly opposite was the yawning mouth of the Missouri river. The Park's shore was lined with fishermen, several of them Black, who helped us heave the canoe up a bank of sticky mud. They were the first Blacks of the journey with whom we had more than the most cursory contact.

We dumped our camping gear at the foot of a monument and went to read the inscriptions on it. On May 14th, 1804, they told us, Meriwether Lewis and William Clark with a party of 43 men had left this place, or somewhere very near it, to travel up the Missouri. They eventually reached the Pacific Coast on November 7th, 1805, and returned to St Louis on September 23rd, 1806. They had covered about 4000 miles on foot, horseback, but mainly by rowing, poling and floating their boats and dug-out canoes on unmapped waterways. Our escapade suddenly seemed like an afternoon outing on the Serpentine.

As a camp site it was pretty awful but I was too busy feeling euphoric at the proximity of St Louis to be troubled by such minor inconveniences as stony ground and general scruffiness. We went to talk to the fishermen. One of the Blacks told us the Park had an evil reputation at night. Some of the kids from the city had parties here. Drugs and drink. Sometimes they got a bit wild and guns were fired. He'd been here once night fishing but wouldn't do it again.

I wished he hadn't told us. We had come to take the friendliness of most riverside folk for granted, inured by distance and time from the ways of big cities. It was an uneasy night punctuated by cars circling slowly along the track round the monument and our tent at the foot of it. Sometimes they stopped, car doors slammed, voices were raised, and for the first time the warnings of our neighbour Steve seemed to have ominous foundation. But whatever these nocturnal visitors were up to no guns were fired, no drunken orgies developed, and at last daylight came bringing with it the first of the new day's fishermen. We got up, stiff and tired, brewed coffee and reloaded the canoe.

The final 16 miles into down town St Louis were memorable mainly for the searing heat and the excruciating snail's pace of our plod down the Chain of Rocks canal. Emerging out of the heat haze two ghostly shapes solidified in painful slow motion into bridges. Once past them the narrow channel between its sharp rock banks continued straight as a ruler into an everafter from which at last a vague blur materialised into something that could only be Lock 27. To our joy a red light turned to amber and, as we got nearer, to green. We had been observed. As the lower gates eased open to let us through unmistakeably southern accents hailed us: "How y'all doin'?" We told them we were all doing fine and, with a wave of our paddles, left the last man-made obstacle on the Mississippi behind.

A mile later we rejoined the main river - still virtually two as the waters of the Mississippi and the Missouri sprinted along, far from united. The currents were fast and very strange and the mounting traffic brisk and business like. As we sped along I registered the sightseeing *Huck Finn*, a plusher cruise boat, a couple of barge convoys, a small tug, a patrol boat. Wherever we were we appeared to be in somebody's way. But there was little time for agitation for the highrise silhouette of down town St Louis seemed to spin towards us and, just before the massive hulk of McKinley Highway and the Railroad Bridge, we edged into a back eddy and pulled the canoe up on the broad sloping wall of the levee.

While George went off to telephone our contact I sat on the edge of the canoe like a displaced water gipsy, tuning into unfamiliar big city sounds and almost ecstatic with joy that we had arrived. Close by the slender curve of the Gateway Arch soared skywards, St Louis' symbolic monument to the great Westward push of the early pioneers.

And for me, I wondered briefly but just then not terribly caring, did it symbolise the great push South - or journey's end?

Chapter Seven.
Towboat to Memphis

In the pilot house of the m.v. *Robert Crown* the marine radio crackled into life. "Mary D. has hit a sand bar at Mile Eleven. Two barges loose on the river. Anyone in the area they'd sure 'preciate your help." The drawl was soft and southern.

"Mile Eleven, that's just north of Cairo where the Ohio river comes in," said our Captain Kenny Dae. I asked if barges often went astray. "Yeah it happens. The river goes down and the sand bars shift. Or someone hits a bridge. They did that in St Louis in the spring. The barges broke loose, drifted off to break up other fleets; there were 175 of 'em loose in the end, going every which-way. That was a real circus."

A few days earlier in St Louis our fortunes and our life style had undergone a swift change and so, I suppose almost inevitably, had my resolutions to abandon the river. To begin with a hotelier friend had lavished upon us all the imaginable comforts we had dreamed of during the more tiresome moments of recent weeks. Dan Mercurio managed the Viking Lodge Hotel, an oasis of calm out amongst the snarling traffic, the gas stations and the 24-hour eateries on the south-west out-skirts of the city. "I guess you could use some space after weeks in a tent," he said ushering us into a suite of rooms in which our Hillsport would have comfortably fitted a dozen times. There were parcels for us sitting on top of the ice box: a T-shirt and a poncho apiece, a huge box of cookies; and a bathroom full of jars and bottles of lotions and creams that held promises of unashamed self-indulgence.

Secondly our friendly contacts at the St Louis Convention and Visitors Commission had put us in touch with a human gem who was to reshape our immediate future. It had always been our hope to hitch a lift on a towboat for a section of the journey and thus experience the river with the true professionals. Now the soft Southern drawl of Wally Rice, one of the Vice Presidents of Federal Barge Lines, affirmed over the phone that arrangements were all in hand for us to ride the Big Muddy for the next 400 miles to Memphis. Next day he took us out to lunch in the elegant Café de France where, against a background of Chopin sonatas and in an atmosphere more reminiscent of Montmartre than the Midwest, he put us in the picture.

"I was real hopeful I could put y'all on our flagship," he said. "But she jammed on a sand bank up in Minnesota and is way off schedule. But don't worry, it's all fixed with our friends in SCNO - that's the Sioux City New Orleans line. They've got the *Robert Crown* coming through in a couple of days - can't say for sure when - I guess y'all know by now how this river can be."

We did indeed. We also knew that Federal Barge Lines had been intimately concerned with the phenomenal development of cargo traffic on the Mississippi. Now privatised it had originally been launched by the Federal Government at the time of the Depression. Massive investments having been poured into the construction of the lock-and-dam system it still remained to be shown that river transport was a viable commercial operation. Wally couldn't (or wouldn't) confirm a story we had heard that, back in those early days, barges had been filled with water so that they sat low in the river encouraging the belief that the profits must be rolling in. True or not it wasn't long before new companies were jumping on the floating bandwagon.

"A good story," Wally agreed, "but the first I heard tell of it. It's a different ball game now though, with the railroad and the tow companies scrapping for what business there is. I guess we don't love each other too much. And that's not to mention the big investment boys who've muscled in ready to cut their prices in the scramble, and not too worried either about operating a tax loss. It's real cut-throat out there on the river these days. It's OK for bigger companies like ours, but the smaller fellas have been feeling it bad - they're selling up all the way down the river."

The cut and thrust of boardroom dealings was a completely new angle for us on our big lonely river. But Wally wanted to know about our journey and smiled or commiserated as our tale unfolded.

"You won't hardly recognise that river when you get back on her again," he said when we had finished.

I looked at him doubtfully. "Is that good or bad?"

"It's just different. Easier in some ways no more of those locks and dams. I guess you know from here on she just rides free. You'll need to look out for the dykes, and there are some strange currents. But when you've come this far, there won't be anything you can't handle. Of course the tows'll be bigger - up to 40-50 barges, but just leave 'em plenty of space. You're not likely to meet one like this though." He fished into his brief-case, producing a newsaper cutting and photograph with a tinge of pride. "That's the biggest baby ever on record: 82 jumbo barges covering over 13 acres. Yeah, she's one of ours."

Two hours sped by and it was time to go. We tried to find the words to thank him for the immense trouble he was taking for a couple of unknown foreigners, but Wally merely shook his head. "When y'all are doing what you're doing I guess you need a shoulder to lean on at times," he said. And after a moment, "And I guess I'd like to be doing what y'all are doing anyway. I'll call you when I've got the timing for the *Robert Crown*."

While we waited we did some of the sights of St Louis where a tiny fur trading post on the Mississippi's west bank had burgeoned as the push West swelled into a mighty drive. Laclede's Landing, as the original site is still called after the young

French trader who established it in the 1760s, could already count over 1000 inhabitants by the dawn of the 19th century. Then came the Louisiana Purchase of 1803 and suddenly the huge and empty acres of the North American continent west of the Mississippi were up for grabs. Native Americans and immigrants from most corners of Europe flooded into this major gateway to westward expansion.

Laclede's Landing, right by the river in down town St Louis, had been tidied up, its cobbled streets and once dilapidated warehouses now smartened into restaurants, craft shops and boutiques and buzzing with visitors. It lay almost in the shadow of Eads Bridge, completed in 1874 and the oldest surviving bridge over the Mississippi. Only a few hundred yards away the slender curve of the Gateway Arch soared up from the river bank, a monument to the pioneers, adventurers, rapscallions and a lot of just ordinary folk seeking a better life. From here they had embarked on journeys whose outcome might be heroic or tragic or full of rich rewards, but almost certainly imbued with considerable discomfort. At the foot of the Arch the excellent Museum to Westward Expansion told us some of the story. But I found my heart was not really in it. The enormous expanses of continent that lay between us and the Pacific seemed somehow remote and irrelevant. For me, now that old resolutions had been abandoned, the Gateway Arch had a quite other significance, marking the transition from the Midwest of Yankee America to the steamy deep Confederate South.

But whichever way you were heading there were no better views to be had of the city and river than from the top of the Arch. We bought our tickets and climbed into one of the cramped little cubicles that bore us in a long series of jerks up to the top where from curiously angled windows we gazed the 630 feet down. Even the big tows were reduced to playthings, the scudding water smoothed to a shimmer; our canoe must have seemed an absurd speck crawling across the grey sheet of the river.

On either bank as far as we could see were the barge terminals that made this America's second largest inland port. In the steamboat days the sternwheelers and sidewheelers were stacked side by side all along the waterfront. When a fire broke out in the *White Cloud* in 1849 it spread to 22 others in no time. Then it reached the one carrying 200 tons of gunpowder and the ensuing explosion set the whole city shuddering and sparked an inferno that raged for four days and three nights while the citizens battled helplessly against it. Only two buildings survived, the old Cathedral and the old Courthouse on whose steps slave auctions were once held. Both in Greek Revival style they added a touch of old-world nostalgia to the glassy high rise of the modern city.

We did a sightseeing trip on the *Huck Finn*, ticked off several museums and wandered about Forest Park where the World Fair was held in 1904 to celebrate the centenary of the Louisiana Purchase. In between we kept in touch with Wally about the progress of the *Robert Crown*. "Be ready at half eleven tomorrow morning," he said at last. On that final evening Dan took us to The Hill, an area of town where his Italian ancestors had moved in in the late 1890s and where everyone still gravitated for the best Italian food.

We had left our canoe in the care of the St Louis Fuel and Supply Service, almost under Macarthur Bridge. It was one of a number of companies that kept the tows supplied with everything from matches to machine parts. Dan came to see us off and so did a couple of local television reporters firing questions at us as we scrambled over cables and bollards loading the canoe and ourselves on to the supply boat that was to ferry us out.

And at last we were waving to Dan's receding figure as we headed out to meet the *Robert Crown* and her fifteen barges mid-stream. As we eased alongside matching our speed to hers several pairs of hands bodily transferred the canoe and our equipment on to a deck that seemed astonishingly spacious from close quarters. The supply boat edged away, the waters between us widened. We were back on the river - and this time in style.

It was in style, too: a comfortable cabin with shower and a small lounge area just outside by the companionway leading up to the wheelhouse. A man with a pink, craggy face and grey hair thrust out a hand. "How y'all doing? I'm Kenny

Dae. It's sure good to have you with us." *Captain* Kenny Dae, Jake the Mate informed us as he led us down to the galley where Ida would "fix us up with some'in to eat."

Everyone had told us that they ate like kings on board the tows. If Ida were any advertisement for her own culinary skills we were certainly in for some feasting. She was enormous, so enormous that many times we marvelled at how she managed to manoeuvre round the well-equipped but compact galley. Gigantic size was a characteristic we had registered early on among a notable proportion of Midwesterners. The reasons, we were told, were rooted in a life style that went with the old frontier days when men and women laboured indefatigably to tame the wilderness and secure a future for their families. They needed to eat, and they ate. Such onerous conditions had long gone, at least for the majority, but the eating habits had not. We had seen that for ourselves in the huge restaurant portions we could never cope with and that had turned us into unashamed users of doggy-bags.

Though it might undermine the quality of life, size was apparently no handicap in the marriage stakes for time and again we saw the slenderest of men or women with the most enormous partners. Certainly it had made no difference to Ida's prospects for she was soon telling us all about her daughter.

Indeed we grew very fond of Ida who greeted me with "Gee, it's great to have another woman on board", and promptly put before us huge hamburgers of a perfect succulence and a salad of ultimate crispness. She hovered over us to make sure we ate every scrap before producing a dream in creamy desserts. "Y'all want coffee?" she then asked. "Help yourself. Any time. It's brewin' all day and all night. My boys make sure of that."

Meals were timed to match the needs of the crew, ten of them working six-hour shifts on a round-the-clock routine. "Supper at 5.30," Ida pronounced, "Lunch at 11.30, breakfast 5.30."

"Ouch," I said, and Ida's large cheeks creased into a broad smile. "I guess I'll find y'all some'in whenever y'all show up."

For the next three days we wallowed in a life style that seemed nothing short of hedonistic. It wasn't just Ida's cooking, though this soared to ever greater heights. It was the sheer joy of non-responsibility for anything that happened, the total unconcern for whatever might lie round the next river bend, the freedom to survey the next storm cloud with interest rather than all-consuming anxiety. And then there was the bliss of the air-conditioning from which I would make occasional forays out on deck soon to be sent scurrying in again by temperatures approaching 100°F. with a humidity to match. The days beyond Memphis didn't bear too much thinking about.

When we weren't feasting in the galley we spent most of our time in the wheelhouse talking to Kenny Dae or the tow's pilot Fred Hunter, a lanky fair-haired Missourian. They seemed happy to yarn for hours, one ear cocked for the messages crackling over the marine radio, eyes constantly attending to the river, the depth finder, the swing metre and, at night, the amber sweep of the radar. And we could certainly have listened to them for ever. Below us our fifteen barges of wheat and soya bean, to which we soon added another twelve, stretched for a quarter-mile ahead. They looked about as manoeuvrable as a tank in a china shop.

Just as in the days of Mark Twain today's river pilots had to be able to draw every inch of the river charts from memory. There were, of course, less snags than in those early times but instead an infinite number of markers for both navigation aid and hazard, every one of them to be stored on the human computer of their minds.

"Before you're ever allowed into the wheelhouse, though," Fred told us, "you gotta be a deck hand for at least three years. A lotta the deck hands are guys making their way through college; others just like the life, don't want the responsibility and are happy to stay down there. But even when you've done your three years it's right up to the Captain whether you get into the wheelhouse or not. A mean captain can make or break your chances. I was lucky."

Fred had married a towboat cook and together they had set up a smallholding; now they were saving to build a new house, so his wife was back on the tows again. They were also enthusiastic canoeists. "Not on the Big Muddy though. We keep to the small fast rivers."

From the solid security of the wheelhouse with the comforting hum of 7000 h.p. behind us, I was having my own thoughts about the Big Muddy. She had become, as Wally Rice had foreshadowed, virtually another river as she prepared to lash her way through the southern states. In St Louis we had picked up the book of navigation charts for the Lower River. They showed her as an endlessly uncoiling serpent, no longer baulked by locks and dams, free of the bluffs which had helped contain her for hundreds of miles, twisting and probing in search of new ways to confound the efforts of a considerable body of engineers entirely dedicated to the task of controlling her.

Over the centuries with fearful regularity the Mississippi has burst her banks and sent her swollen waters raging over thousands of square miles of the southern states, drowning plantations, communities and very many human souls. Once she was recorded as 80 miles wide and covering an area half the size of England. Time and again she has shifted her course, sometimes by scores of miles, more often forcing a short cut across the narrow neck of one of her own hairpin meanders to leave yet another community high and dry and scattering the soggy landscape with oxbow lakes, now the haunt of fishermen and wild life.

Today the Mississippi's freedom is far more conditional. Revetment reinforces hundreds of miles of the river banks against erosion. Hundreds of miles more of levees form an irregular but almost continuous line from the junction with the Ohio River at Cairo much of the way to the Gulf of Mexico. Mostly they stand well back from the tangled forests of willow and cottonwood that extend back in every stage of vigour and decay from the river banks. Constantly under review, repair and reinforcement the levees provide the final line of defence against the worst excesses of the river. Behind them lie the vast plantations of cotton or soya bean that replace the wheatlands of further north, with here and there an occasional farm or community. Our future life on the Mississippi promised to be very lonely indeed.

The charts also marked a new potential hazard for canoes: a line of dashes leading out at varying angles and great frequency

106

from one or other bank. These indicated the presence of wing dams, called dykes on this lower river, designed to direct the greatest flow of water out into the navigation channel.

"What about those?" I asked Fred as we throbbed past one and I noted the water churning angrily over a broken line of rocks.

"No problem," Fred said, "as long as you keep away from that turbulence at the end of 'em. Just stay well out in the river. Only watch out for us tows of course." It sounded a counsel of perfection.

Below us Jake and a couple of the deck hands were working their way round the barges in the sweltering heat. Night and day much of their routine was dedicated to checking the couplings that lashed the barges into a rigid raft. It needed sure footwork edging along the exposed outer sides of the cargo holds and it was mandatory to wear a p.f.d - personal flotation device, the new jargon for an old-fashioned life jacket.

"It doesn't help any, though, if you fall off while the tow's moving," Fred told us. "You just get sucked in and pinned underneath." He was luckier when he fell off in his deckhand days. Somehow his p.f.d. got ripped off and he emerged from an all-engulfing blackness not far from land. "It was two in the morning," he said, quite without drama. "Once I managed to crawl ashore I just lay there, must have been a full half hour, before I could even stand up my legs were shaking so much. There was a bridge close by, so I made for that. They'd already reported me a goner and called the Coast Guard."

I found my own legs shaking at the very thought. "You must be like the cat with nine lives."

"Yeah, I guess so." He added "I think this job's great, but that's the only thing that worries me - the responsibility for those other lives. It only needs a very small bump to send someone over the side. And there's a lotta potential for bumps."

Indeed it was hard to imagine anything more unwieldy than a Mississippi tow and we never ceased to marvel as we watched Kenny or Fred go through the infinitely delicate process of negotiating contortions in the river that not infrequently achieved 180 degrees. If there were other traffic in the area there would first be crackling consultations over the marine radio, the combination of atmospherics and variations of southern drawl making them virtually incomprehensible to us, though we got the general gist.

"I'm at 895, north of Winchester Towhead and holdin' back while you come through," one message might indicate.

"Sure 'preciate that Cap'n. Startin' to back up now."

Or, equally, the priorities might be reversed. It was odd to associate those spluttered human sounds with something as apparently intractable as the gigantic bulk of floating hardware that would eventualy nose into our field of vision and slide past a score of yards to port.

With the channel clear we would head rather unnervingly for the outer bank of the bend. When it seemed we must be at imminent risk of hitting it the flanking process would begin, with engines in reverse, letting the river slowly nudge our solid acreage round. Forward again, and then reverse, forward, reverse. It could take an hour to back up round the tighter of the bends when the current was tricky.

Once as we were coasting down a rare long straight stretch Fred grunted at a small dot bobbing up and down directly in our path. "Crazy fool. Doesn't he know it takes me a mile and a half to stop in this current," he said and blasted a warning toot at what materialised into a fisherman oblivious- ly checking his lines right in the middle of the shipping channel. "Yeah, he's jug fishing," Fred commented as we watched the man frenziedly collecting up his equipment before scurrying out of our way. "They put out plastic cartons or cans with a line and bait, and let 'em go with the current. When they gotta catch, the cartons or cans are pulled upright, and all they gotta do is haul 'em in."

We told him some of the problems we'd had with the weekend motor boat brigade. "They're the worst," Fred agreed. "It's nothing for them to come in close to ride the wash, or cut across just ahead of me. Why, they'll even do it with water skiers in tow. If one of 'em falls off, or their engine dies, there's just nothing, nothing at all I can do. You hear of terrible tragedies." The thought of them made Fred look as angry as we ever saw him.

On another occasion he said "One of the things I love about

this job is that no two trips are ever the same - depth of water, sandbanks, current, wind, weather, the combination is always different."

George asked him if he had ever got caught in the ice. "Yeah. Last winter was really something. Normally you'll get loose ice down as far as Natchez; last winter she was solid all the way to New Orleans. When there's a lotta ice we form up into a mule train, with the tow hauling instead of pushing, the barges spread out in a single line from about 200 feet behind. But when it's real bad the ice piles up into a massive wall moving with the current the full width of the river. That's when you get outta the way and find a hole somewhere in the bank to lie up till it's passed. I've seen those ice walls spread back a mile and a half. They bring the Corps of Engineers in then to break 'em up with dynamite."

It was the night watch Fred preferred. "It's just you and the Big Muddy then," he said and when we shared his lonely night vigil we understood why. The dark river was another world then of black shapes and winking navigation lights, of searchlights probing the ebony shore or picking out the channel buoys. Periodically over the marine radio he reported his position to other captains, exchanged brief jokes or news. But somehow the loneliness out there crept right into the secure oasis of the wheelhouse and the sense of his alertness was almost tangible.

The hours and the miles slipped effortlessly by. Out there beyond the air-conditioning Illinois on the left bank abruptly ended as the Ohio river poured in to join us. At the junction we stopped briefly at Cairo to drop off some barges and pick up others. Here technically the Lower Mississippi began. We had reached Mile 0 for traffic heading north and Mile 980.8 for those destined for the Gulf of Mexico. I did a quick calculation. Good God we weren't even half way. From Memphis there would still be 736 miles to go.

"How about staying with us to New Orleans?" Kenny said. But I knew there wasn't a hope.

Missouri persisted on the right bank; on the left we were now in Kentucky, our sixth State and the only one we would not set foot in. On the second evening we passed New Madrid, still in Missouri and a reminder that it was not only tempest and flood that had bedevilled the early settlers. In December 1811 a series of earthquakes of fearsome proportions hit New Madrid, plunging it into the river and so transforming the configuration of the valley that the original site of the little community ended up on the opposite Kentucky shore. The present town is back in Missouri at the head of one of the Big Muddy's most famous double loops, a 20-mile bend that is only 1000 feet wide at its base. It's nobody's wish that the river should ever find a way across this heavily reinforced narrow neck for the resulting surge of current would have consequences too dire to contemplate.

By night fall we had already crossed from Kentucky into Tennessee and down in the galley Ida was marking up a long list of groceries. Kenny would radio her requirements through to the marine supply service in Memphis and it would be ready and waiting for delivery when we arrived.

"I'll miss y'all," she said. We'd spent a lot of time chatting, Ida and I, over countless cups of coffee from the ever-brewing pot. Early on I had come upon her poring over fat journals and learned of her all-abiding passion for genealogy. She had already made remarkable headway in tracing her ancestry back to the England of pre-*Mayflower* days.

"Mebbe one day I'll be calling y'all from some place in one of your shires," she said, a little wistful at the unlikelihood of it happening. I hoped she would.

We left the *Robert Crown* midstream as we had boarded her, stepping on to a tug from Waterways Marine Inc. that had eased alongside at matching speed. There was swift, brawny activity as crates of Ida's groceries and mechanical hardware for Jake were exchanged for our canoe, its load and us. Final thanks and farewells were bawled above chugging engine sounds, a channel of water widened between the two vessels, and the tug turned away to head for the shiny geometrical forest on the left bank that was down town Memphis. The joy-ride was over.

We had radio telephoned our estimated time of arrival. Amongst the clutter of cables on the wharf of Waterways Marine a reception committee awaited: a TV crew, radio reporter, and a beaming welcome from Sharon, delegated to be our guide and mentor. She was pretty, intelligent and Black, and the instant empathy between us was happily mutual.

Camping was obviously out of the question so we settled for a down town hotel. In the few minutes drive to it there were fleeting first impressions of the city of the Blues and of Elvis Presley, world capital of cotton. A lot had obviously changed in Memphis since mules strained up and down cobblestoned banks between the cotton warehouses on Front Street and the fleets of paddle-steamers lining the waterfront, the first leg of a journey that would end in the textile mills of Europe. But it was still the largest spot cotton market in the world and, if the romance had gone, so had the sweated labour.

We checked in and headed for Sharon's office in Beale Street, on the way passing Elvis Presley Plaza and Handy Park and a statue apiece honouring these famous citizens. Even we had heard of Beale Street, not only as home of the Blues but as a rough-and-tumble place where knives and guns were easily drawn and, if you were White, you stayed away. The tidy street of restaurants and boutiques and cafés was not at all what we expected. We took Sharon out for a coffee.

"Sure, we've made it respectable," she said, "Y'all could bring your grandmother here now, no problem. And plenty of cops around to see it stays that way." We had noticed those too. We knew instinctively that we could ask Sharon anything. Her shoulders appeared singularly free of any chips.

"Guess I'm a real cocktail," she first explained. "Half Black, quarter Cherokee, quarter German. My husband, he's Black and we have two sons. One Blacker than me, the other as fair as any German. That's a real problem for him to know just where he belongs. I worry for him."

So as we drove around the city, out beyond the down town high rise into amorphous suburbs of shopping malls and residential areas where barred windows and doors spoke volumes about the crime rate, we told Sharon about our hopes. How practical, we asked, would it be in the Southern States to meet Blacks on more than a casual basis - in their homes, attending their churches, for example?

She shook her head. "It's not gonna be easy. I guess it's

gonna take a long time for things to change. You can change a law, but people, that's something different. You go into a church for Blacks and you're the only Whites, they're gonna wonder what you're doing there. Maybe you've gone to laugh at them." George began to protest but she shook her head again. "Sure, *you* know you're not going for that reason, but they won't understand that. It's better you don't go except you get invited by a Black. And I sure don't know how you'll get to fix that."

"But surely," I said. "There must be times when Blacks and Whites mix socially."

Sharon considered this. "We work together, joke together, study together and all that stuff. But really socialise, no. Well, of course there are exceptions; maybe quite a lot. But we mostly live in different areas, have our different meeting places. Sure you'll see Blacks and Whites in the same theatres, hotels, restaurants, but it's not too often you see them at the same table."

I was saddened by her certainty but hoped perhaps we would prove her wrong, though her answer to George's next question was even more disturbing and discouraging. Scrawled on billboards he had noticed the sinister initials of the Ku Klux Klan.

"I guess racialism under whatever umbrella it operates is a bit more subtle these days," Sharon said. "Top people in the big corporations wield a lotta power, and you won't find too many Blacks in those positions though you'd have a hard time proving why. In some of the backwoods areas of the Southern States bigotry is still pretty bad. Yeah, you can still hear of lynchings - but nobody's gonna stick their neck out and call it that. And who's gonna prove it? Poverty, drugs, alcohol, these things breed violence whether you're Black or White, and who's to say the real reason when someone gets beaten up, or worse, in a brawl?"

We had an invitation to visit Graceland, the 18-room mansion set in 14 acres of grounds that had become a shrine to millions of Elvis Presley worshippers. I was glad we did not have to join the considerable queue at the door. People whose opinions I respected were adamant that he was a great creative artist who had changed the entire course of pop music. I prepared therefore to forget my musical prejudices and open the doors of my mind.

The music room was dominated by a huge 24-carat gold-leafed concert grand piano. There was a Jungle Room full of ersatz animal skins, spears, and dark green carpeting covering most of the floor, walls and ceiling. Down in the basement TV room, a mirror ceiling reflected blue clouds on bright yellow walls and the three 25-inch television screens built into one of them so that the King of Rock and Roll could watch three programmes simultaneously. In the Trophy Room glittering costumes were on display and an entire wall gleamed with gold and platinum records representing the hundreds of millions sold. Out in the car port Elvis' mother's pink Cadillac stood among a fleet of shiny cars and flashy motorbikes. We reached the Meditation Garden and its family graves just ahead of the next onslaught of visitors.

Despite all efforts my open mind was having a hard time to find the values represented by the place and its shuffling queues of reverent fans anything but intensely depressing. The young idol who had died such a wretched death in early middle age may have created inspirational sounds but I searched in vain for anything remotely admirable in the material remains of the life style that went with them. I appealed to Sharon.

She did not hesitate. "He left his music and that's *great*; it kinda gave a whole generation a new identity, and that's the one I grew up in. And he was generous in an almost crazy way. Would see some poor old woman on the street and give her a Cadillac, that sorta thing. But some other things seem real sick - though it's hard to dig out truth from legend." She shrugged. "Guess you could say that about a lotta famous folk." And we left it at that.

We escaped from Graceland's reverential crowds with relief and, with some irony, noted the rather sparser human presence that afternoon on Mud Island, just across the inlet from the wharf of Waterways Marine. Here, on a 50-acre slab of once weed-infested mud the outstandingly good Mississippi River Museum had recently been created. Detailed documents, maps, plans, prints and models were supplemented by full-size replicas complete with sound effects. In an 1870s luxury packetboat we eavesdropped on passengers' conversations on yellowfever epidemics and the latest fashions from Paris. Nearby a Union gunboat was engaged in noisy duel with a Confederate shore battery, and in the River Folk Gallery life size characters told what it was like to live and work on the river. It was "instant Mississippi" but extremely well done.

Outside there was a River Walk along a replica of the entire Lower River: 1000 miles from Cairo to New Orleans reduced to scale to a thousand paces or five city blocks. We strolled along its minuscule waters, stepping over New Madrid's 20-mile bend, across scores of capes and islands to reach the labyrinthine channels of the delta. A stone's throw away the Big Muddy herself rolled implacably on to disappear, beyond a railroad bridge, round one of her innumerable meanders as we were scheduled to do next day.

But first we went that evening to the old cotton warehouse that had become Blues Alley and, over barbecued ribs and baked beans, listened to the magic sounds whose origins were rooted in the hollers, the heat and the sweat of the cotton fields. Sharon could not come but "You'll hear the real thing at Blues Alley," she told us. "Just listen, watch - and feel."

So in the heat and smoke of packed humanity we listened to the impeccable rhythms and we watched the faces of their creators, charged with fervour, glistening with sweat; and we shared the emotions as Ma Rainey II and Little Laura Duke, both long past retirement age, expressed love and jealousy, laughter and aching nostalgia with every fibre of their venerable beings, while the guitar, the sax, the trumpet and the trombone throbbed and sobbed or jubilated in the same message. Pinned up on the wall behind them were photographs of the great Blues masters and, almost the only White, the unmistakeable features of Elvis Presley. "He must have had something," I whispered to George. "This lot certainly do." We left emotionally quite drained.

As we packed our bags back at the hotel we saw ourselves on TV for the first time.

"Pardon me," the very young interviewer had said to George "But don't you think you're rather old for canoeing the

Mississippi?"

"It could be," George replied, "that some people would be too old at thirty."

But infuriatingly, the programme's compère had the last word.

"Aren't they just great? I know y'all wanna join me in wishing the best of luck down the Big Muddy to that elderly British pair...."

Chapter Eight
"Anyone lost a canoe?"

Amidst a clutter of boxes and crates on the wharf of the Memphis Marine Service we embraced Sharon. There was a suspicion of tears on her dusky face. "I think you're very sexy," she told George and directed her beaming smile at both of us.

Massing clouds surged out of the northern sky, their blue-black matching my mood at the prospect of getting back on the river. But the gods had other ideas. Attached to the canoe was a message scrawled in pencil on a page torn from a notebook. "Dear Intrepids," it began. "If you feel like lunch or dinner or whatever, come over to the *Connie Mays* at the Lone Star Cement Wharf next door. Just completed a solo canoe journey of 6,700 miles. It would be good to talk." Signed Ted Layton.

We found Ted - a lean, weathered and bearded British-born Australian - cabinet-making on board the *Connie Mays*. She was one of five old tow boats saved from the scrapyard by a Kentucky millionaire known as Red Mays because of his taste for red clothing. Each vessel had been or was being completely refitted before going back into service. Ted had first encountered the outfit on the *Sherry Kay Mays* back in the winter.

"They sort of kidnapped me off the river around Cairo," he explained. "I'd spent Christmas in a cave down a side creek in temperatures way below freezing. The river was completely iced up - something almost unheard of so far south. After a while I got back on the river but was still having trouble with ice floes, and it was pretty damned cold. They invited me on board the *Sherry Mays* for a meal. Didn't need asking twice! Then they found I was a bit of a carpenter and somehow that meal stretched into several weeks till the weather warmed up. We met up again on the Intracoastal. I got a ride back and now there's this boat to work on. So here I am."

I wondered whether he had been born with that enviably relaxed approach to everything that came his way or acquired it on the kind of adventure he had just completed. Solo, Ted had canoed the Mississippi system from and to its ultimate, paddling from the source of the Milk River in Montana's Glacier Park to join the Missouri and thence the Mississippi down to New Orleans, and finally along the man-made Intracoastal Waterway into Texas. All told it had taken a year and a half. We could only feel humble admiration.

Ted confirmed what we had already heard from Wally Rice and observed from the wheelhouse of the *Robert Crown*: the Lower River could be a very, very lonely place. Together we pored over the charts marking some of his favourite camp sites on the peppery expanses that represented the sand bars.

"Carry plenty of water - it can get *hot* out there. But you shouldn't have any problems. There are quite a few barge terminals and places where the levee comes close to the river. If you get up on that you'll maybe find a farm on the other side." (In fact, we never did). He thought for a moment. "Be careful on the levees though. Have you got boots?" We hadn't. "No, well take a stick along. Some of the snakes aren't too friendly if you tread on 'em by mistake. There was a water moccasin that gave me a bad time."

A lot of people had uttered darkly about snakes, even seemed surprised we weren't carrying any serum; but then some had been even more amazed at our lack of firearms.

"What happened?"

"Not much I could do really except use my belt as a tourniquet, then slowly release it every 20 minutes or so to control the poison getting into the blood stream. I knew it would be OK after the first few hours, but it took about four days before the swelling spread up the leg and started going down again and I could walk a bit. Fortunately I'd got plenty of supplies." He grinned. "Every time a boat went by I'd wave and yell, but if they saw me they just waved back, all friendly. I think that was the worst time." But he added reassuringly, "It really was my own fault. In this part of the world you just don't go walking through thick vegetation without boots or a stick."

We sat in the small galley yarning away happily over the remains of cold meat and salad. Members of the crew came and went, all "sure happy to meet y'all" and exchanging banter with Ted. We had almost forgotten why we were there and what we ought to be doing when a zip of lightning was followed rapidly by a crash of thunder, and a curtain of water fell out of the sky.

"Why not stay on board for the night," Ted suggested. "I imagine you're not too worried about luxury?"

I tried not to look hopeful. "Good idea," George said.

We yarned some more, then the rain eased a little and we scurried out to salvage the sodden contents of the canoe. None too soon either for we had moored her to a barge that was now being unloaded and slowly rising out of the water. That evening Ted introduced us to Charles, the *Connie Mays'* captain, the most self-contained and unassuming of men who was quietly adamant that he would move out of his cabin for us. Over supper he asked a lot about our journey and I was just embarking on our encounters in Nauvoo when I caught a certain look on Ted's face and at the same registered that Charles neither smoked nor drank tea or coffee.

"You're a Mormon?" I said, and he smiled and nodded. Not that there was anything remotely offensive I would or could have said about our stay with those delightful people, except perhaps repeat my bafflement at stories of inscribed gold plates mysteriously revealed, transcribed and lost again. To this sceptic Charles' gentle manner and enviable aura of a man at peace with himself served as a much more effective argument.

Next morning he was insistent that in future we must have

our life jackets, if not actually on our backs, attached to us at all times while on the river. A member of the crew was delegated to prepare two lengths of rope, spliced at both ends round a solid bolt that would guarantee security. Charles' final gesture was to present me with a copy of the Book of Mormon.

Seventy-three miles of river stretched between us and Helena, Arkansas' only river port and our next point of contact with civilisation. We estimated it would take three days and had provisions for four. It was, as yet, the longest period when there would be no remote possibility of pulling in to a small-town supermarket or a riverside tavern for the delights of iced drinks and air conditioning. But for the moment heat was not a problem. The series of storms had freshened the air and the breeze was fair. The current was fair, too, and despite a late start we did an easy 20 miles before pitching up on a sand bar.

For all our theoretical knowledge of the changed character of the river it was quite another matter to experience the reality. We might have been on a totally different expedition. During the next three days there were few moments when we were not either profoundly aware of the river's altered mood or learning something new about her behaviour. There had been plenty of lonely stretches further north, especially in the sloughs, but the empty enormity of these horizons and the certain knowledge that any human contact was virtually inaccessible across soggy swamp and forest or acres of cotton beyond the levees, gave the loneliness a very different quality.

The currents were quite different, too, and sometimes extremely odd. No longer baulked by dams the river dictated its own pace. We got to know where the fast water was: on the outer side of the interminable bends, or more or less down the middle of the rare straight stretches - though there were puzzling exceptions enough to prove these rules. On the inner sides of the bends the water sometimes came virtually to a standstill and we might as well have been paddling through treacle as we crept round the sand bars sprawling out far from the shore. Some of them were vast like mini Saharas stretching to within a hundred yards of the opposite bank, occasionally ribbed by tempting channels that might offer a short cut, or, just as likely, bring us to a dismaying halt as we grounded in waters too shallow even for our negligible draught.

It was not always possible, and sometimes downright undesirable, to be in the fast water. That was precisely where the tows were likely to be and on a tight bend, caught between steep revetment on one side and expanses of sand on the other, you were left with little time and space for manoeuvre. Once we encountered a tow of 56 barges, high in the water and obviously empty, heading upstream; most of them were somewhere between 25-35 barges and I tried not to think too nostalgically of those halcyon days when we saw them from a quite different perspective from the wheelhouse of the *Robert Crown*.

Our most testing times, though, were with the jagged rocks of the dykes. In the high water north of St Louis all of them had been submerged, even those marked on the charts as normally exposed. Now they were all completely or half exposed, and the latter were infinitely the more trying for they were impossible to see from the low level of a canoe. More often than not the first indication of the wretched things was the sound of rushing water. The charts marked their position but did not indicate their length since, as far as motorised traffic was concerned, their choice of route was clearly limited to the confines of the port and starboard markers. The dykes also caused the currents to do some peculiar and uncomfortable things. In most cases where the fast flow of water met the obstruction it would swerve into reverse in a series of swirling back eddies, while immediately upstream of the dykes it virtually came to a standstill.

Remembering Ted's recommendations we adopted the practice of heading out for the channel markers, having first checked that no tows were imminent. Usually the markers were placed well clear of the end of the dykes, but it was not always so and at this point the turbulence ranged from the negligible to the horrendous. Never at ease at the best of times when we were far from shore I found each avoiding tactic dismaying.

The worst occasion, however, was on the third day when we encountered a dyke that, according to the charts, was not there. Later the Corps of Engineers agreed that it had only just been constructed, confirming the advisability of having the very latest charts. Our first indication of it was of a faint sound, for all the world like the hum of a distant factory. Ahead we could see a dredger spewing out water from its rear and river silt through a long pipe, and briefly thought that this must be the cause. But as the hum increased to a faint roar and then to the worrying sound of a cascade, we now saw the tell-tale irregular white ridge that could only mean water breaking over rocks.

"We'll head up and mid-stream," George said tersely, and with every ounce of strength we did just that. The current was fast and now the roar of water and the sight of the cauldron foaming viciously over jagged rocks became very alarming indeed.

"We won't do it, it's impossible," I whimpered, sick with fear and already anticipating the physical pain of the last moments before oblivion. Then the nearest rocks slid by within inches. For interminable moments the jagged chaos seemed hungrily poised to draw us in. And then, noticeably, they were receding and I knew that on this occasion at least we had survived.

Once in calmer water I peered angrily at the charts. "It wasn't supposed to be there. I wonder how many more little surprises like that are in store for us. Bloody river. Bloody charts."

George wisely ignored me. Neither of us was at our best for the episode came on top of a particularly lousy night. Storms had threatened intermittently since we left Memphis and the previous evening had fulfilled their promise, eventually erupting around 11.30 p.m. The tent was pitched securely enough and we were relatively sheltered in a small gulley. But there was a new lesson to be learned.

When the storm finally broke it was of the full-blooded Mississippi variety and no messing. I had developed by now a kind of resignation to this all-too-familiar bombardment of one's senses and lay in the stifling heat amidst the flashing and crashing accepting, with however much bad grace, a situation I could not change. Then I became aware that on George's side of the tent all was not well. And so we discovered we were pitched half on pure sand, half on a thin layer of sand over dried mud. Sand can absorb a vast amount of water very rapidly; dried mud merely becomes wet mud, and George had just found all our cooking utensils and most of his personal gear sitting in a rising tide of glutinous pap.

We hauled as much of it as we could into the inner tent and when the storm retreated to a grumbling distance around 2.30 a.m. finally dozed uneasily. At 6 a.m. it was still raining but we mopped up as best we could determined to reduce the remaining 26 miles to Helena as quickly as possible. Progress was hampered by head winds but at least the extraordinary contortions of the river now meant that in the time it took to negotiate a 180 degree bend a head wind would be transformed into a helpful shove from the rear. We chose a route that avoided dykes as far as possible until we came across the one that should not have been there.

After that Helena became the most desirable place on earth and the few remaining miles among the longest and weariest of the journey. Hot, dirty, tired to the marrow, and with paddling arms working like automatons on the blink, the final two miles seemed to stretch to eternity as we scoured the right bank for the necessary landmarks.

"Turn right into the inlet just before a barge terminal," Charlie Fite of Helena's Chamber of Commerce had told us when we rang him from Memphis. "About a mile before the bridge. You'll see our small-boat marina - can't miss it."

Accustomed to the busy little marinas of the Upper River we could be forgiven for not easily identifying the deserted and steep muddy embankment as Helena's equivalent. But as far as I was concerned it had all the attributes of paradise as we hauled the canoe out and squelched up the slope to the little shack that served as a tavern, with the ecstatic prospect of at least two days ashore. And at that stage we didn't know the half of it.

"Got a meeting on, be over as soon as I can," Charlie said when I called him from the tavern. "It's great you got here." Later we learned that in his concern for our peculiar venture he had sent a boat out looking for us earlier that day.

Half an hour later George had just gone to start unloading and I was still rooted in weariness to the bar stool when a young woman approached. "Hello, I'm Maureen Jones, and you'll be staying with us," she said in tones originating beyond any shadow of doubt from the Home Counties.

We had experienced hospitality of an overwhelming nature from individuals all the way down the river. Now we were about to be taken over by a whole town. On the way down to the canoe we met a burly man in a pair of old jeans carting up some of our mud-spattered gear. "Bill Brothers," he said, holding out a large hand. "Just came along to make sure y'all doing fine." A car screeched to a halt. "There's Charlie. See y'all later."

Maureen, blessedly perceptive, firmly blocked all proposals that we should "meet a few folks that evening". "You're exhausted," she stated rather than questioned, and bundled us into the car as soon as the canoe had been man-handled into the tavern's store room for safe keeping. My dim memories of that evening are of nodding quietly over a superb meal to which I could not possibly do justice before falling into bed in the charming room that the Jones's had vacated for us, despite all protestations.

Over breakfast we consolidated the scraps of information half absorbed the previous evening. Maureen's husband Neville was in charge of a chemical plant having become disillusioned with boardroom politics back in the U.K. Maureen had a part time job at the Episcopal Church. Earlier that morning she had already attended the weekly breakfast arranged by the church for the under-privileged. Their two children, fast losing their Home Counties accents, were at local schools.

"Bill Brothers has arranged a party for you tonight, and Charlie's showing you the sights today," Maureen said. "You'll probably find the sheer volume of kindness as overwhelming as we did. We just got taken over as soon as we arrived - I just couldn't believe it was all happening to me and kept waiting for it to fizzle out. But it never has. The difficult thing is that never in a million years can you make it up. Not that anyone expects or wants you to, but you know how you feel." We did indeed.

During the next 24 hours we got to know more people in Helena than in several years in our own home village. A high proportion of them were guests at a party which Bill Brothers and his wife, Cassie, arranged for us at their home that second evening. It was a beautiful home, the livingroom lined with books and full of treasures from many parts of the world; but there was little time then to examine them.

"Hi, I'm Martha (or Janet or Marjorie or Mary-Ann), and this is my husband John (or Jake or Matt or Eddie). We're so excited to meet y'all and so thrilled at what y'all are doing. And we wanna know *all* about it."

Increasingly dazed I bounced from one group to another, feeling like a human gramophone that had got jammed on "repeat". George had vanished but returned some time later to explain he had sneaked off with Bill to be shown the "yard" beside whose swimming pool a small chalet was designed as charming self-contained guest accommodation. Bill, it seemed, had put it at our disposal for whenever and as long as we liked, an offer that we were to value rather sooner than we dreamt. It was at this point they had also discovered that in the 1940s they had mutually fought their war within a few miles of each other in Egypt.

As time went on we surmised from snippets gleaned here and there that Bill was more or less the uncrowned king of Helena. A Canadian that had "gone bad" as Cassie would teasingly tell him, he had stayed on in the States after the war and gone into crop spraying, in due course switching from this dangerous but lucrative occupation to trucking. From this he had expanded into a multiplicity of activities whose reins he was now ostensibly handing over to his son, but on which he nevertheless seemed to retain a rather firm grip. As we were driven round Helena by Maureen or Charlie or Bill himself almost every corner produced a factory, warehouse, motel or piece of real estate which once had or still featured in Bill's empire. Out in the countryside the soya bean and cotton plantations of Cassie's family covered vast acres.

All the same huge tracts of swamp and primeval forest still survived out there to show what the whole of that countryside had been like before the then French territory of Louisiana had been so casually sold off by Napoleon in 1803. Much of it had subsequently been apportioned to farmers displaced by the devastating New Madrid earthquake up river in 1811, or to soldiers in return for services rendered in the war of 1812.

Drawing its wealth from the cotton plantations and its bustling life from the river Helena, like many another, had withered for a while with the passing of the steamboats, and time and again suffered appalling floods. Now there were more recent industries and the town lay behind high levees, secure but almost invisible to passing river traffic. Approaching by road you might never know the Mississippi was there unless you took Highway 49 across the great steel and concrete bridge, the only one in over 200 river miles between Memphis and Greenville, Mississippi.

As elsewhere the stores and banks and real estate offices, the gas stations and eateries, had mostly moved out to the shopping malls away from down town. Closer in the beautiful homes and gardens of the White community nestled, well spaced out, along the little lanes that rose and fell among hills sub-tropical in their profusion of trees and vegetation. A few of the houses actually qualified as "antebellum" (pre-Civil War), a word that was to become very familiar on our progression south. Ambivalent in its attitudes towards this bitter conflict, Helena and its surroundings had supplied the Confederate Army with seven generals and later been a victorious Unionist stronghold.

In the old down town area that crouched behind the levee, though, life was noticeably returning to the newly restored 19th and 20th century buildings along thoroughfares like Cherry and Perry Streets. It was a different scene only a few blocks away in the shanty town where, almost without exception, every face was Black.

I've forgotten the percentage of Black population in Helena, but it was high as in all Southern communities. "We encourage 'em all to stay in one place and they can fight and kill each other as much as they please," someone commented, and I was about to protest at the sick joke when I realised they were not intending to be funny.

In rare spare moments during the journey I was reading *Gone With the Wind*, thereby repairing a long standing omission and trying to reach some understanding of attitudes that still prevail in practice, if not in law, among many Southerners. Yet many of the very same people who from time to time propounded views that were quite preposterous to us devoted a great deal of effort and not a little money to good works directed to the under-privileged of both races. Towards individual Blacks who worked for them the deeply caring if paternalistic attitude of White employers might have been a mirror image of the South I found in the pages of Margaret Mitchell. It was just as Sharon, back in Memphis, had said it would be.

Almost the only Blacks we were to speak to anywhere in the South were in shops and offices, unless we took the initiative ourselves when the occasion arose, usually in large cities. In smaller communities there was virtually no common meeting ground for social contact. In Helena the only Black with whom we had any close dealings was Willy, the Brothers' glorious old retainer, wrinkled as a prune. She had been with the family for decades, was indeed considered part of it, and confided with surprise to Cassie "Ain't folks just the same wherever they from? That English couple seem real frien'ly tho' I can't understan' a word they say!"

So should we offend our generous hosts by expounding our own views evolved from much travel and friends of many races but from actually living in a community where a Black face was an interesting novelty? Shamefully we opted for the easy way and kept quiet.

At some stage in our social whirl Maureen took us off to meet a rare woman. Lorena Connaway was a widow who grew pecans and lived alone in a rambling old house. "I guess it's a bit untidy," she said, not seriously apologetic. "But there are always so many more interesting things to do."

It was a one-woman natural history museum. Every shelf and surface displayed some neatly labelled collection of items excavated from the bed or banks of the Mississippi: samples of sand, stones, rocks, fossils, plants, insects, small reptiles. There were bottles of coloured sand layered into patterns; landscapes made from more coloured sand stuck on to pieces of board; sculptures composed of driftwood and stones; arrangements of dried plants and grasses.

Lorena told us her son was an archaeologist. Sometimes he would take her on an outing, scouring the sand banks for new treasures. "We find all kinds - sharks' teeth, fragments of bison bone, stones carried down by the river from as far away as the Great Lakes." Rummaging amongst the splendid disorder Lorena produced thick books of press cuttings relating to every aspect of the river's history, topography, economy, traffic. "It's so sad when you hear people doing terrible things because they're bored. How can anyone be bored when life is so interesting?"

The enthusiasm might have sounded ingenuous but this was a very practical lady. Still rummaging she found a stack of notebooks full of the neat sloping hand in which she had kept detailed records of the recipients of various missions of mercy: a family of purple martins, a mocking bird which "had a different call for each member of the family", a quail, a prothonotary warbler - "a real back seat driver, that one." Another notebook carefully recorded the usefulness or hazards of local plants: thus may apple and may pop merited "Use fruit ONLY ...rest POISONOUS."

Studying the list I said "I see that kudzu has its medicinal value."

Lorena grimaced. "They surely made a mistake with that one. That's what happens when you fool around with nature." Kudzu, imported from the Orient, had been planted all over Helena and other parts of the South to halt soil erosion. Now it rampaged up hill and down dale, engulfing all before it in cascades of pretty green that apparently turned an awful brown in winter. But basically Lorena's firm philosophy was that everything had its purpose and its place.

"I'll try and remember that in the next diabolical storm," I said wryly.

We left her reluctantly. "Such a pity it's not the pecan season, but I'll send a parcel." She hugged us both. "I think y'all are the nicest thing that's happened this summer..." She presented us with a plastic bag full of wild herbs. "These will keep the mosquitoes away."

The time came to leave Helena. On our last evening I thought uneasily of the 126 miles of winding waters, lonely sand bars and banks of tangled growth that lay between us and Greenville, Mississippi. We had stocked up with a week's food, bought an extra water container, and a cooler that would keep us in ice for at least the first 24 hours.

About a dozen people came to see us off, including the Jones's, Lorena, Bill and Charlie, and reporters from the local paper and radio. It was a bit of an anticlimax when we found the tavern closed and our canoe inaccessible. One of the reporters went off to put a message out over the radio and in due course the tavern owner arrived, but by then another storm was imminent. Like farewells prolonged at a railway station when the train is delayed our well wishers were running out of things to say, and so were we.

We encouraged them to go and pick up the threads of their daily lives, covered our canoe with sheets of plastic and went off to visit a couple of young men from Iowa who had just arrived in a houseboat. On board everything was meticulously organised: bunks, work bench, desk, cooking area, and every tool and utensil precisely placed. Over freshly brewed coffee they told us how they had salvaged the hull of a Corps of Engineers vessel, built the houseboat themselves and were aiming eventually for South America. It was good to exchange tales of discomfort and elation with fellow travellers who knew the Big Muddy from similar close quarters.

The rain eased and we left at last at 1 p.m., and such was the series of events that led to a change of plan with very dismal repercussions. Twelve miles downstream from Helena was an institution called the National River Academy where young men and women with an ambition to work on the tows could learn all aspects of river skills from cook to master pilot. It was, we were told, the only one of its kind in the United States. We had met its director, Tom, at one of our many social gatherings in Helena. "Why not drop in for a meal," he'd said. "Or stay the night. You can't miss it if you pull up on the sand bar below the levee about a half mile from the Academy."

We had checked the charts, originally with the idea of calling in for lunch, and it did indeed look quite straight forward. Now, following our late start I suggested we took Tom up on his offer of a bed for that night.

"We'll see," George said non-commitally.

It was not after all easy to find. From a small canoe on a big river one stretch of sand bar or levee covered with bushes and cottonwood trees looks much like another. We did the 12 miles in good time and as we approached a tree-covered promontory where sand was abruptly replaced by revetment decided to beach. The levee which had looked so close lay a good half mile back behind sand and scrub. When we eventually reached the top of it we looked out over an endless acreage of soya bean and, in the middle of it among a group of trees a mile and a half away, a lone building that could only be the Academy. The way was shadeless and the afternoon at the peak of its stifling heat, but by now we were sufficiently committed and George too was dreaming of long cold drinks.

In his air conditioned office Tom was delighted to see us. "Come and have something to eat," he said. "Then I'll drive you back and you can paddle down to a much closer sand bar so you can get off to an early start in the morning."

A couple of hours later he dropped us near the canoe. "How will we recognise the right place?" I asked. "It all looks the same from the river."

"I'll be waiting for you," Tom said. "No problem."

It took us about twenty minutes to slither through the sand back to the canoe, push off and round the promontory. Beyond it was a small beach. "No Tom," George said, "Can't be that."

But as we continued in a quickening current alongside a steep bank of revetment we finally knew that it must have been "that". There was no question of paddling back against such a current and no option but to land somehow and make a reconnaissance. Landing on the steep revetment was extremely difficult and getting the canoe out of the water quite impossible without additional muscle power. We moored her to rocks and scrambled to the top to be faced by more endless acreage of soya bean and not a building in sight. And dusk was falling fast.

"Try and get back to that beach," George said. "I'll make the canoe as secure as I can and follow on."

I stumbled off along the edge of the soya beans, heading

for the trees that marked the promontory now a good mile back, bawling Tom's name, flapping away at the gathering mosquitoes and remembering the snakes. On a distant track I saw the lights of a vehicle heading for the promontory and stumbled faster. By the time I reached it I was sweating profusely, gasping for breath and trailing a cloud of mosquitoes. But at least the vehicle was still there and I eventually got a response from Tom crashing about in the undergrowth below.

"Gee, I'm sorry," he said. "I reckoned it would take you at least an hour and went back to finish off a few jobs."

"It was less than a mile," I protested, but there was no point in labouring the matter. George was almost speechless when he caught up with us. But we were as much worried as angry for it was now almost dark and the canoe was moored far from the track in a place where no sane canoeist would dream of leaving their craft overnight. Tom was reassuring. "The shipping channel is way over on the other side of the river," he said. "The canoe's in deep water; it'll be OK."

There was another deluge in the night and even I viewed the prospect of a long slog back through soya beans to a saturated canoe as a high price for a night under a roof. But it was worse than that.

We were just about to leave after an early breakfast when the Coast Guard arrived.

"Anyone know anything about some canoeists?" they asked.

"That's us," we said, full of foreboding.

"Praise be y'all are OK. But your canoe was found upside down. The Marine Service have taken it back to Helena, along with some stuff they found floating in the river..."

Chapter Nine.
"She just keeps rollin'"

My first reaction was: thank God, I need never get on that river again. The second was engulfing dismay at all that wasted agonising and effort. Despite his tan George managed to look grey with despair as he said bleakly "We might as well pack up and go home." So it was my turn to be the optimist and I heard myself firmly making the unlikely statement "Nonsense, we can't possibly give up now. We've still got the canoe. All we need are the paddles and a few essentials."

A tow had been exchanging barges, the Coast Guard explained, just a hundred yards from where the canoe was moored. In the darkness they had not seen it. Nothing was actually said about the insanity of leaving a canoe in such a place, and it was futile to start apportioning blame. I could just imagine the turbulence from those screws and the canoe tossed in it like a leaf in a waterfall. The miracle was that she had not broken away from her unorthodox mooring and disappeared for ever.

Tom, very subdued, said "We'll go check the shore." We went by truck bumping along the levee to the nearest point, but there was still a mile of muddy slog through drenched soya bean. I kept thoughts of snakes to myself and remembered the Dordogne escapade when we had spent a day scouring the river banks on foot and further downstream by car, retrieving a motley collection of our belongings caught up on overhanging branches or washed up on some beach. Here we were restricted to slippery footwork along a limited stretch of revetment. An hour's search yielded a life jacket and an assortment of plastic containers.

The real moment of truth came later that morning when, back in Helena, we stood waiting on the wharf of Helena Marine Service. One by one the salvaged and sodden remains of our expedition were man-handled from tugboat to shore: the canoe, two of our three paddles, the aluminium box, tent, kitchen box, the other life jacket. We began to dare hope. As we levered the lid off the aluminium box I could hardly breathe. We poked about inside, looked at each other in marvelling disbelief. All George's camera equipment, films, my journals of the journey, stoves, first aid kit, sleeping bags, our "best" clothes - and not a drop of water. George's face was a joy to behold.

It was about to rain. We dragged everything in to the shelter of a shed and went up to the office to list our losses: one paddle, the mattresses, water containers and ice cooler, the several days food we had just bought and, saddest of all, my rucksack. Most of its contents - spare clothing, toilet things - were easily replaced, but I remembered with a pang a few items of jewellery including my wedding ring.

The office secretary plied us with sympathy and coffee while we tried to track down Bill Brothers by phone. We were still trying when a call came through and, after a brief exchange, the secretary said with a broad smile "I guess this is for you."

Mystified I listened to a voice at the other end of the line saying he was Johnny Williamson from Elaine, a score of miles down river. He'd been fishing, he said, when he suddenly noticed something floating down on the current - our roll of mattresses. "Then along came a backpack. That seemed kinda strange, but I fished it out and when I opened it and found the jewellery and the English dough" (£50 - I'd completely forgotten that) "I figured somebody'd be mighty glad to have it back. So I came on home and called the police, and they said to call here. Sure am glad I found y'all."

I could only stammer gratitude, still hardly believing my ears. "Yeah, well my Pa and me have to come in to Helena, so we'll be with y'all in a half hour." He was about to ring off when he had an afterthought. "Oh, and my Ma's right now washing them clothes but I guess there won't be time to dry 'em off. See you."

There was a click. I reported to George then burst into tears.

Soon after we got hold of Bill. "I'll be there right soon" he said as we barely finished spilling out our tale of woe, and arrived with a truck within the hour.

The tale was to be repeated many times in the next three days as Helena once again absorbed us into a cocoon of kindness. Bill and Cassie had installed us in the chalet by their swimming pool. Systematically we hosed, brushed, scraped, laundered and/or ironed every item, and then went off with Bill to hunt through the shopping malls for replacements of missing essentials. Only a spare paddle eluded us.

Bill took it for granted he would drive us to Greenville "so y'all can catch up on your schedule." I was joyous at the prospect of leap-frogging well over a hundred river miles and so we loaded up the truck again and headed across the bridge and out over the old flood plain of Mississippi State. Locally everyone referred to these ancient bottomlands as the Delta which, indeed, they probably once formed. What it meant in historic terms were some 30,000 square miles, from Cairo right down to the Gulf, regularly subjected to flood and the resulting layers of millions of tons of Mississippi silt. Now all of it lay within the protection of the levee system.

"That's one of the richest top soils in the world," Bill commented as we drove across the endless expanses of cotton and soya bean plantations. Then added thoughtfully "But no more floods means no more silt. We have to keep up the fertilising now. Ironic isn't it?"

It seemed you just couldn't win with that river. Certainly the citizens of Greenville had paid their share of the price for any favours the Mississippi had brought them, for the town had twice been gobbled up and, in the big floods of 1927, it stood under water for 70 days. That was before massive improve-

133

ments in the levee system and before the Corps of Engineers gouged out one of their cut-offs, diverting the river on to a straighter course. Now Greenville lay 5 miles off the Mississippi up the narrow still waters of Lake Ferguson that filled part of the old river bed.

We stopped off in down town Greenville to make contact with Jenny, our young and pretty mentor from the local Chamber of Commerce. Bill, who had an eye for pretty young ladies, showed a marked reluctance to leave but declined an invitation to join the welcoming party that Jenny had laid on for us that evening. We never did get used to the impact our escapade seemed to make on riverside towns, punctuating our lonely days on the river with interludes of frenetic social whirl.

After the party we were taken to one of the most famous eating houses on the Lower Mississippi. "You'll find it kinda basic," Jenny warned us and, indeed, the undecorated walls and bare scrubbed tables at Doe's Eat Place provided a décor as modest as its name. But there was nothing at all modest about the steaks which were Doe's speciality, none of which came under 2 lbs in weight. We shared two of these between six of us, preceding them with shrimps in lemon and garlic. It was still far too much and we watched amazed as diners at neighbouring tables launched into a full-size steak apiece.

Greenville had been a major port for transferring cargo from river to rail. The old railroad complex was currently up for restoration and development and the rambling 1890s depot already housed a restaurant. Once removed from the mainstream of the Mississippi, however, Greenville had become a fine slack-water harbour with dozens of tow companies and boat building and repair yards lining the shore, until the recession began to bite. We spent next morning at the office of Brent Towing Company. With its sister Marine Supply and Shipbuilding enterprises it was one of the biggest on the lower river. "Used to be touchin' thirty tow companies along this bank," Howard Brent told us. "Now I doubt there's ten."

We repeated what Wally Rice had said back in St Louis. "Yeah, the investment companies priced a lot of the smaller guys right off the market, then bought 'em up. It was tough.

But you can't fool around too much with this river. Now the situation's turnin' and they're findin' losin' money ain't so convenient. Like a mouse in a trap - they don't want no cheese no more; they just want out."

"So what happens next?" I asked.

Howard shrugged. "Just now the railroad companies ain't too happy with us and have bin makin' a lotta noise lately. They wanna buy in - that's not bin allowed before. Accordin' to them we've all had it real easy on the river - free use of them expensive locks, and all the money poured in to stop her breakin' loose. But you don't hear 'em braggin' too much about all the mineral rights they're sittin' on, nor all them acres of land." He grinned. "Ain't nothin' simple when it comes to the river."

Greenville's population was predominantly Black, but signs of integration were as difficult to find here as in Helena. On our second evening Jenny took us for drinks with "probably the only Democrat in town."

Jerry Nash spelled out what had happened when integration was finally imposed on schools in the '60s. "The Whites just took their kids away and put them in new private schools that sprung up like mushrooms. I guess you can imagine the effect that had on the general level of education."

"Not all the Whites," Jenny said. "I told my folks I didn't wanna quit my school, and most of the other White kids stayed as well. It worked out fine. But I guess that didn't happen too often."

George was curious. "What made you decide to stay?"

Jenny shrugged. "I dunno - it just seemed to make sense." She added "My family are die-hard Southerners in their way of seeing things, and that's the way I was brought up too. They find it real hard to understand why I think the way I do - that it's the way people are that matters. They can't figure where I got these ideas, and I don't know either except, like I said, it seems to make sense."

With a few more Jennys around at least there was hope for change.

A big supermarket shop next morning yielded a spare paddle, but it was past noon when Jenny dropped us off at Waterways

135

Marine where we had left the canoe close to the junction of Lake Ferguson and the Mississippi. Every interlude off the river seemed to make the idea of getting back on to her more unappealing and the churning anxiety had been building up all morning. The river had dropped further leaving steep banks of mud to negotiate. It was a windless day and diabolically hot. As Jenny turned to go back to the busy affairs of her air-conditioned office I felt as though the last tenuous link with normality was being severed again. Ahead lay the limbo of a life dictated by the whims of the river. I glared at her rolling implacably by and became very busy organising my end of the canoe.

Once committed to the water and heading out into the current I reverted to my old fear-blocking habit of counting paddle strokes. One hundred, two hundred, three hundred ...that many more achieved, that many less to go... with relief I emerged from dark thoughts to find that at least the canoe and the river were in harmony, and behind me George was chuntering happily about the joys of gipsy life. It was going to be all right, of course it was. Benevolently the Big Muddy bore us along for 18 miles before presenting us with one of the loveliest camp sites of the whole journey.

For the next 300 miles we could be confident that camping problems at least should be over. As impediments to speedy progress the sprawling sand bars and accompanying shallows on almost every bend were frustrating; but as camp sites they offered an almost unlimited choice. Ideally we would hope for one that was not too expansive, giving quick access to the forest rim beyond. Trees gave the double benefit of shade after long hours of unbroken exposure to the sun and a degree of protection from strong winds which continued to bedevil many of our days, though ironically they did frequently ease with the approach of evening.

We were not, of course, always lucky. There were times when the shelter of even the most modest vegetation lay half a mile or more from the tent. For practical purposes this had to be pitched as close as possible to the canoe which we would draw well out of the river, unload completely and then turn upside down. We had long ago learned the rashness of assuming that a calm fair evening would necessarily be followed by a calm fair night. It was much easier to unload and have everything within reach of the tent's protection than to face the tiresome mopping up operations required by even the briefest deluge.

Similarly we learned to look out for tell-tale moist runnels in the sand that could turn into a muddy stream in a matter of minutes in a cloudburst. I was also now insistent that we tested the sand thoroughly before landing for in Greenville we had learned of yet another of the Mississippi's idiosyncracies: quicksand.

To the unpractised eye a firmly established sand bar looked much the same as the shoals constantly shifted by the restless forces of the river. Only a short time earlier a local family had suffered the tragic loss of father and child as a firm crust of sand collapsed into the treacherous hollows eroded beneath it by the current. Several times well out into the river we grounded on such shoals and despite our mightiest efforts with the paddles failed to push ourselves free. There were uneasy moments as we got out of the canoe to pull her into deeper water, the sand almost instantly sucking us in to above the ankle. Once George said "There's no need for us both to get out."

"If she's going to get one of us, she might as well get us both," I said cheerfully, but wasn't entirely joking.

All the same there were evenings on those sand bars that were near perfection. Then our small tent with the canoe drawn up nearby became our own private little pocket of civilisation in a world totally dominated by the river. Occasionally a jonboat would buzz past carrying a fisherman to his nets or jug lines. Or a motor launch or cruiser rumbled by rising high at the head of its own trail of turbulence. But our most constant companions were the tows, remote in their preoccupation with the narrow thread of the navigation channel. With dusk the shore markers began winking out their port and starboard messages to the throbbing black shapes whose searchlights would flicker across the tent from time to time on their lonely journey through the night.

These were the times when the river was truly ours and

137

I found myself thinking back to our predecessors of long ago whose craft, as subject to the bidding of the Mississippi as our own, nevertheless had turned her to their own purposes and made of this wild waterway one of the great colonising and trading routes of the world.

The most primitive of them had been the ark, little more than a raft with a rudimentary shelter built 'amidships', and well named for it was by this method the first families and their livestock had travelled down the Ohio river to settle the middle Mississippi valley. Many a prosperous plantation had its origins in an ark tied to a tree by a clearing freshly hacked out of the forest. The more substantial flatboat was essentially a cargo carrier: anything from flour and furs to lumber and lead, cotton and cattle to salt and slaves. The long steering oars slanted out either side from the flat roof of the covered shed that sheltered the cargo. Later I found an extract from a Southern lawyer's diary of the 1830s that showed things had not changed much on the river.

"The whole course of the Mississippi is only a series of bends; therefore, on turning points the utmost vigilance is necessary to work the boat and keep it out from the bank against which the natural direction of the current would carry it. When the wind blows hard against the shore, the utmost exertions of the half-dozen muscular men who form the complement of flatboat-men cannot always enable them to counteract the forces of both wind and current and many boats are dashed to pieces..."

For both the ark and the flatboat any journey on the river was strictly one-way only. At the end of it the craft was broken up and the crew had to find their way back the best they could. The keelboat was a different matter and the gaudiest, bawdiest stories are associated with these vessels and the legendary activities of their brawling, roistering crews. Up to 120 feet long a keelboat needed a crew of 8-15 men to control it downstream and more than double the number to negotiate the return trip, poling against wind and current on journeys that might take 3-4 months from New Orleans to Pittsburg on the Ohio. In the riverside ports along the way, saloons, bordellos and gaming houses blossomed to cater for their favourite relaxations. Some, like Mike Fink, became cult figures celebrated in ballads and poems for their wild adventures and, like him, their colourful lives ended not unusually in violent deaths.

As for us, our 'ports of call' had more peaceful distractions. Evening and early morning brought small groups of waders or skeins of wood storks, early migrants on an age-old route through the continent, winging out of the sunrise or sunset. Once we shared our sand bar with a miscellany of waders far too busy with their own affairs to be concerned either by our proximity or each other's. Neat, slender, spotted sandpipers, already changing into soft olive-brown winter plumage, pottered about in the pools indifferent to the cumbersome short-billed dowitchers jabbing at the mud with the rhythmic precision of a sewing machine. Several lesser yellowlegs balanced among them on long thin yellow legs.

"Remember the last time we saw one of those?" George said. But I was already indulging in nostalgic memory of a lone specimen that had strayed far off course to our local sewage farm and caused a mighty stir among Oxfordshire birdwatchers. Overnight the smooth sand around the tent would become patterned with claw and paw prints, some in purposeful straight lines, others exploratory meanderings, telling of much activity from invisible companions while we slept. Sometimes we heard a grunt or snuffle but were never quick enough to glimpse its owner.

Our hopes that the sand bars might be immune from the nightly ritual of mosquitoes proved alas, ill-founded. With clockwork regularity about 45 minutes after sundown we detected the first unmistakeable whine, precursor of the onslaught that would follow within seconds. With camp routine now down to a fine art we were ready for them, the meal over and cleared up, the tent organised for our hasty retreat. We would then lie sweating until the hum of their countless millions reached its zenith. But the Mississippi mosquitoes on the whole were more obliging than their Danube counterparts, for in due course the astonishing volume of noise would ease and we would put cautious noses out into the night. With luck we were able to take the air for a while before turning in, and those were some of the best moments of all.

Eventually the night also brought relief from the heat and humidity - especially the humidity. Temperatures were now daily in the mid to upper 90°sF, but it was the humidity that made conditions so awful. By 10 a.m. we felt for all the world as though we were paddling through a Turkish bath. By lunch time, drained of all energy we were scouring the banks with our binoculars for a safe mooring for the canoe and shade in which to lie up for a couple of hours. It was not always an easy combination to find. Once in mid-afternoon desperation we pulled on to a sand bar and scrambled barefooted towards the nearest trees, a good 500 yards away. We had forgotten how effectively sand absorbs heat; it was like walking over hot coals and kept us hopping and "ouching" all the way.

The greatest penance of all, certainly for George, was dehydration. I don't sweat much and suffered accordingly more from the heat; but George who sweats profusely went through torments of thirst that could be quite worrying. Following local advice we always carried a supply of Gatoraide in soluble powder form which, we were told, was composed of the constituents of sweat and therefore replaced all the essential minerals lost in profuse sweating. Fortunately it was available in a variety of fruit flavourings and was refreshing as well as effective. Certainly it put an end to painful cramps.

All the same we looked forward more fervently than ever to our ports of call which were now few and far between. In the 500 miles between Memphis and Baton Rouge they could be numbered on the fingers of one hand: Helena, Greenville, Vicksburg, Natchez and the ferry landing at St Francisville. Happily we had excellent contacts in our tenth and final State of Louisiana who, more concerned for our welfare than we initially realised, made arrangements for us to be looked after at two off-river communities in order to break up our longer port-less stretches. The procedure was for us to pull in at a specified barge terminal on the river bank from which we would telephone to announce our arrival.

Thus our introduction to Louisiana was via the muddy banks beneath Lake Providence Port Elevator. The little town of Lake Providence itself was a mere mile as the crow flew from the river bank, steep with revetment at this point. But the only access to it was 1½ miles up an inlet to the port installations from which a dirt road led the 2-3 miles into town. It was a rotten place to land and a long hot wait until we finally got our message through to the right person, but at last a slender gentle woman materialised and agreed she was indeed Gayle Brown.

"Y'all must be so hot and tired," she said as she drove us deftly into down town Lake Providence. "It's so wonderful what y'all are doing."

"Good Lord," exclaimed George. And Gayle smiled and slowed down so that we could fully appreciate the message in flashing lights that winked out from a screen in front of a bank on Main Street. "Temperature 94°F ...17th August ...Louisiana welcomes British canoeists George and Sylvie ...Temperature 94°F ...17th August ...Louisiana welcomes British canoeists..."

"We're having a little party later," Gayle said. "I guess we mustn't wear y'all out, but there's so much to show you and everyone's so excited about your visit."

There was indeed a party with a magnificent cake someone had baked and decorated in icing with our names and a picture of a canoe. Afterwards in golden evening light Gayle drove us round the shores of Lake Providence itself, a real Mississippi ox-bow where we saw our first cypress trees rooted in the water. And later the comings and goings continued at the comfortable rambling house on Lake Street. Everyone was overwhelmingly kind, enthusiastic and admiring. I felt achingly tired and a terrible fraud.

Gayle had seven daughters. The two youngest were totally fascinated by us and our accents, asking every few minutes if we would like a cold drink or a cookie simply for the joy of hearing us speak.

"I guess they were a bit nervous about your visit," Gayle admitted when she got to know us better. "Y'all are the first foreigners they've met and it was kinda hard to explain that people really are all the same wherever they're from. I'm real happy the way they're relating to you."

Equally important was the way we related to Gayle, one of those rare people who comes as near to being truly good as one may hope to meet on this earth. Suddenly it was all too much. I found myself pouring out to her all my fears and inadequacies and, horror of horrors, bursting into tears through which I burbled a plea to stay on another night.

"We'd be so happy if y'all would," Gayle said with an accompanying hug to confirm it. "See, there's no shame in being afraid. I can't tell you how much I admire what y'all are doing. George too of course, but I guess men are a lot tougher than we are after all." And for once I did not try to dispute it.

While George had a ride in a crop sprayer, flying out over the river to get aerial shots of tows, I spent most of our blissful extra day sleeping. It was the ideal therapy.

As we left Lake Providence next morning a tug boat chugged past us only to pause hovering at the exit of the inlet.

"Wish he'd decide where he's going," George was saying irritably when from the tug a voice boomed out "We wish y'all a safe and happy journey."

We had been aware of a haze as we left town but now on the main river we got the full impact of the grey shroud that drew a veil across the opposite bank and reduced visibility up and down stream to a rather worryingly few score of yards. Listening carefully we could detect no tell-tale throb of engines but we were right in the navigation channel.

"Better nip across while the going's good," George said.

The current was extremely brisk as we paddled vigorously across it at an angle towards the invisible sand banks marked on our charts on the opposite shore. And it was then without warning that we hit our first "boils". Vivid descriptions of these phenomena had been contained in every account written by our predecessors on the river, and it was surprising we had not encountered them before. Their cause was the passage of fast water over some irregularity in the river bed. Their effect was tumultuous as the water erupted explosively and without warning all around us into raised "boils", often many yards across. Alternating with these were whirlpools in which the water spun in ever-decreasing circles to disappear, as it were, into its own centre.

It was all extremely disconcerting as the We-no-nah veered

and swung at the river's bidding. I remembered what Mike Chichanowski had said in far away Winona, Minnesota: "Don't look at the water, but ahead at the horizon." Well, there wasn't much horizon to be seen. But with some relief I found this was one danger that proved more apparent than real. With our shallow draft we skimmed out almost as quickly as we were drawn in to these strange excrescences, aided by the appropriate strokes which George soon developed to a fine art.

Nevertheless it was an uneasy morning for the thick haze made navigation through a particularly complex area of sand bars very difficult, and it was a great relief a few miles later to come out of the haze and into a more familiar set of topographical features: revetment, sand banks, cottonwood trees ...and then more of the same.

The sand banks sprawled out from the inner curve of almost every serpentine bend, the river barely straightening out from one before launching into the next. Sometimes they sprawled so far that she was squeezed into a deep swift stream just wide enough for the navigation channel, hard up against the revetment on the opposite shore. These were most undesirable circumstances in which to coincide with a tow but fortunately there was usually plenty of warning as long as we remembered to check in both directions. It could have the oddest effect as an approaching tow's massive bulk apparently glided over the sand behind or ahead, foreshadowing the inevitable wait as it went through the complex back-up procedure that we had witnessed so often from the wheelhouse of the *Robert Crown*.

Indeed there were moments of special nostalgia that late afternoon as we made camp on a sand bank and the *Robert Crown* rumbled briskly by along a rare straight stretch of the river. We "halloo-ed" and waved wildly but there was no response, and we guessed most of the crew just then were concentrating on Ida's gastronomic delights. George rummaged in the food box. "And what would Madam like tonight? A tin of stew ...or a tin of stew?"

There were a lot of tows on that section and more significantly on the second day a marked number of jonboats, a clear indication that we were approaching our next major port of call.

Vicksburg lay about a mile up the Yazoo River which met the Mississippi on a sharp bend. We had to pull hard out of the fast waters and even harder to make any progress against the Yazoo's current, modest though it was. But from all we had heard Vicksburg merited at least a three-night stay and that thought alone was enough to add extra muscle to my elbow power.

And at the junction we had passed a marker: 437.3 miles to go. Maybe, just maybe, we might make it after all.

Chapter Ten
Stormy Times

At 2.10 p.m. on April 26th, 1876, the Big Muddy finally broke
through a narrow neck of land opposite Vicksburg and once
and for all turned its back on the city. Before long the old
river bed had silted up. It was a quarter of a century before
the Corps of Engineers diverted the tributary Yazoo past Vicksburg's
front door, thus restoring to it access to the commercial life
blood of the Mississippi.

"The great irony," Benita said as we stood on Walnut Hill
looking down on the Yazoo and the distant shimmer of the
Big Muddy, "is the river did all by herself what General Grant
and all his Unionist forces couldn't figure how to do. With
Vicksburg commanding the Mississippi it was a real no-go
situation for a while."

Just how much of an irony we learned over the next couple
of days. Had the river done her deed a mere 13 years earlier
there would have been no need for the Siege of Vicksburg,
no resulting 22,000 military dead, no starving or diseased civil-
ians, no devastated buildings.

Within a very short time of arriving in the little city it became
abundantly clear to us that, as far as Vicksburg was concerned,
only one war had ever really existed. Everyone's time scale

related to it and it was as if no war had happened before or since. When events or buildings were described as "before" or "after" the war, it was taken for granted you knew the war in question was the Civil War - or the War Between the States as Southerners more usually called it. Architecturally it was a watershed. Buildings were either antebellum (pre-war) or not; the actual style was a secondary detail.

Our own Vicksburg *pied-à-terre* just missed qualifying as antebellum. Like many others of similar vintage Flowerree did a high class line in b. and b. Benita, who had come to collect us from the public wharf soon after our arrival, drove us straight there. There was a swimming pool and we were to stay in the luxurious garden guest house which, like the main house, was stuffed with antiques, many brought from Europe. For two water gipsies fresh from the river it was like wonderland.

Over dinner that evening we established an immediate rapport with Benita and her husband Larry. Larry was immensely keen to take my place in the canoe for a few days, and I was immensely keen to let him. "While y'all are gone I'll turn Sylvie into a real Southern Belle," Benita said enthusiastically. But, alas, there was no chance to find out how she intended to achieve this unlikely feat for Larry's job made the whole delightful prospect impracticable.

In 1863 Vicksburg had dominated a giant horseshoe bend in the Mississippi and, with it, a vital line of communication between Unionist forces to the north and south. The bend itself was rather young having only been created by the river's whim less than two score years earlier, and it had already caused some testy exchanges between the States of Mississippi and Louisiana over boundary rights. Alarmed by Louisiana's plan to cut a canal thereby diverting the river and grabbing back its disputed territory, Mississippi passed a law in 1858 of eloquent ineffectiveness:

"That if any person shall make any cut-off, whereby to shorten the Mississippi, or shall dig or cut any channel or ditch, with intent to make a cut-off, whereby to shorten said river or shall attempt to make such cut-off or to dig or cut such channel or ditch or shall clear the brush wood, whereby to shorten said river, or in any other manner aid in making such cut-off or in digging or cutting such channel or ditch, whereby to shorten said river, or shall counsel, employ or procure any person to do or commit any of the aforesaid acts, he shall be liable to indictment and on conviction shall be punished by imprisonment in the penitentiary not more than five years."

Such legal niceties were of huge indifference to General Grant five years later when he set his soldiers and slaves recruited from the Louisiana plantations to dig just such a channel and divert the river away from the shore batteries of Vicksburg. The men worked day and night. But the Mississippi had a different timetable. Diabolical weather, sickness, racial tension and unutterable misery combined to defeat their greatest efforts. Sheer force of numbers proved equally unavailing. Only one alternative remained: to starve the Confederates out.

The Siege of Vicksburg began on May 18th, 1863, and lasted 47 days. The Unionist troops dug themselves in among a network of trenches below the hill town, and inch by inch continued to dig their way ever further up the slopes. Eventually the two armies were so close that when firing ceased in the evening the soldiers from either side exchanged jokes or sought news of friends and relatives until the mutual massacre resumed next morning. As food and water ran out the besieged Confederates, soldiers and citizens, eked out dwindling supplies of rancid bacon and musty pea flour with mule meat. As the bombardment intensified they burrowed caves in the hillsides. Contemporary diaries give graphic accounts of the conditions, though little is said of what happened to the slaves.

On July 3rd the Confederate General Pemberton surrendered and on July 4th Unionist troops entered the city. There was a bitter irony about the date and for over eighty years the people of Vicksburg doggedly declined to join the rest of the nation in celebrating Independence Day.

We spent half a day in the 1800-acre Vicksburg National Military Park where the siege campaign could be followed in the minutest detail in a lovely setting of woods and meadows. Occasionally a jogger panted by, sweating it out in the afternoon swelter. And from a hill we looked out again at the river which had acted too late.

For the next couple of days we rejoiced in the exceeding comfort and hospitality that Vicksburg lavished upon us. The *Delta Queen* was in port so we had the opportunity to see from the inside how the other half lived afloat the Big Muddy. At up to several hundred dollars a day I conceded her passengers deserved the teak, mahogany and walnut wood fittings, the stained glass windows, the luxury menus, the lavish entertainment, and the asthmatic whistlings of the calliope that played her in and out of every port. We did a trip on the Yazoo on the *Spirit of Vicksburg*. We visited the Old Courthouse Museum whose Civil war collections included newspapers printed on wallpaper when more conventional materials ran out. We stuffed ourselves with Southern fare at the Walnut Hills restaurant, built in 1880: Southern fried chicken and corn bread with a dozen mostly mysterious vegetables. We dined on redfish almandine at Tuminello's run by a Basque American. Above all we wallowed in air-conditioning.

"They haven't a clue what it's like out there on the river," murmured George as we transferred from air-conditioned vessels to air-conditioned cars to air-conditioned homes and offices.

But there were two places where we were obliged to broil for a while. One was the Waterways Experimental Station whose technology was to feature prominently in our journey a few days further downstream. The other was 40 miles out of town at Clinton. Here a model of the Mississippi basin, begun by prisoners of war from Rommel's Afrika Corps in the 1940s, covered a 45-acre site. Its purpose was to re-create and observe the effects of floods in the entire Mississippi basin. Not a lot was happening that day for a series of tests on the interaction between the Ohio and Mississippi rivers at Cairo had just finished, and the next - a study of the St Louis levee system - not yet begun. It was just very hot and very quiet, and exceedingly odd to travel in a few paces the remaining miles to the Gulf whose reality would fully occupy us for the next four weeks.

"I'll be thinking of y'all," Benita said as she helped us re-load the canoe on the third morning.

In fact the river gave us an easy time for the next few days except for one or two rather uncomfortably close encounters with tows. One of them in particular reinforced the wisdom of those of our predecessors who had invested in a marine radio. Caught napping in the navigation channel close to steep banks of revetment we had scuttled into the mouth of a small bayou, as we now learned to call the myriad creeks of the Southern states, in order to get out of the way of a descending tow. To our surprise its engines suddenly went into reverse and the massive bulk came to a halt a few hundred yards downstream. For a long time nothing happened. Then another descending tow appeared and eased past it.

Still it did not move. We hovered anxiously, fearful of the turmoil if it got under way as we were passing and aware that the last thing any captain could be expected to look out for in the middle of this Lower Mississippi nowhere was a canoe creeping up from the rear. Two wasted hours passed and we could wait no longer. There appeared to be just room for us to creep through between the tow's starboard side and the revetment, which seemed marginally the better course. Halloo-ing wildly we nudged out of our refuge and sidled along the quarter-mile of barges without mishap and with huge relief.

Otherwise it was mostly all right. To some degree we had acclimatised to the heat and the humidity, or at least endured them with more equanimity. And the camp sites were exquisite, one in particular on firm smooth sand at the foot of a tree-topped bank from whose shade we spent the evening hours watching the river and the occasional tow, completely at peace.

As we prepared breakfast early next morning skeins of wood storks headed down river, some in V-formation, some in straggly lines, the pink flush of sunrise behind them. Altogether that was a good day for we only had 15 miles of paddling to reach St Joseph. Here arrangements had been made for us to get off the river from which it was no longer directly accessible other than by a link road serving the Great River Grain Elevator that loomed beside a particularly muddy stretch of bank. Our hosts were to be Kirk and Bruce who ran a guesthouse.

St Joseph had a sleepy main street and an even sleepier village green set amongst a scattering of antebellum houses. Kirk walked us round it and up on to the levee. In this case it was a second line of defence and looked out, not over the river, but across muddy pools and a tangle of scrub and trees.

"All this becomes a floodway in high water," Kirk explained. "They call it a 'bor pit' - you find them all along the river. 'Bor' that's short for 'borowed' - they borrowed the earth, you see, to build the levees. Great fishing - great for snakes too."

Bruce who worked in a government office, duly arrived home and a photographer from the local paper came to immortalise us relaxing in the garden. It was a leisurely evening over delicious home cooking and talk turned again to integration. Bruce was a New Yorker. "I guess the South was at least more honest about its segregation," he said. "In the north we preached liberality and looked the other way when the opposite was practised. But it's a mistake to think it's one-sided." He told us how they'd tried to arrange a house party for both Black and White colleagues from his office one New Year. "Only two Blacks turned up, and not many more Whites. I guess you could call it a non-event."

Only two easy paddling days remained before reaching Natchez, and I was enjoying an unusually extended mood of optimism. We knew it to be one of the most interesting places on the river and a rare response to our earlier flood of letters had told us to look out for a barge docked down on the river below the bluffs, adding encouragingly "On the street above the barge which is the oldest street in town is a wonderful place called Silver Street Inn which overlooks the river and you are invited to be guests..."

We had rung Carolyn Denton, author of the letter, to confirm our imminent arrival. "Pull in just before the bridge," she said. "You can dock your canoe by the barge and know y'all have reached Natchez-under-the-Hill. Call me when you arrive."

The first impression wasn't quite what we expected. Most of Natchez-under-the-Hill had been gobbled up long ago by the river. Indeed Silver Street was all that remained of it and it needed a fair stretch of imagination to visualise the bustle and clutter that had once made this wharf the busiest and most infamous place in the State of Mississippi. Here in their droves flatboatmen with their cargoes of flour and tobacco, hemp and pork, reached the end of epic journeys from up river. If they were lucky they broke up their vessels and sold the timber; if they were not they simply abandoned them. Either way, before they embarked on the long overland trek back north along the Natchez Trace there were plenty of establishments ready to relieve them of whatever profits they had made - bordellos, gambling dens, dance halls, taverns.

Then came the cotton boom. Steam boats whistled in and out of the Landing, their decks jammed with cotton bales. There were floating wharf boats and coal barges docked side by side and the place pulsated with commerce, high living and villainy, probably in equal measure, amidst the clutter of warehouses and proliferating places of entertainment. Away from it all, up on the green rolling bluffs the fine families in their fine houses grew and prospered.

"They say," Carolyn told us as she drove us deftly round that serene other-Natchez, "that at one time we had more millionaires than any other city except New York."

Their prosperity did not survive the effects of the Civil War but many of their magnificent homes did in varying states of repair, until roads and motorised traffic brought a more lucrative invasion. Natchez rediscovered her heritage and, as someone wryly put it, "opened her doors to the Yankee dollar."

Over 500 buildings of all kinds still qualified as antebellum, and forty of them took part in the Natchez Pilgrimage, a spring and autumn flood of visitors pouring through antebellum homes to learn about the antebellum way of life from guides dressed in antebellum costume. We did likewise and found ourselves right back in a world barely vacated by Scarlett O'Hara.

There was no denying the elegance of those stately piles, built by slave labour and variously described as Colonial, Georgian but, above all, Greek Revival, gracious with porticos and airy galleries. From between Doric or Corinthian or Tuscan columns we looked out over immaculate lawns to profusions of magnolia trees and azaleas, camellias and japonica, and imagined echoes of music and chatter and the rustle of petticoats. Within, we wandered from spacious room to spacious room gazing upon Regency furniture, French mirrors, Waterford crystal chandeliers, Italian marble fireplaces, Oriental antiques, fine silver and porcelain, and the best of craftsmanship available from New York to New Orleans. Then we went of to see the antebellum quarters of servants and slaves. Some had been adapted into natty tourist accommodation which I doubt would be recognised by the original occupants.

But perhaps in the end it was the largest and grandest of all the homes that underlined the illusion of even the most seemingly impregnable security. Within its octagonal walls and beneath its cupola, Longwood House was an opulent unfinished postscript to the antebellum era. Interrupted by the Civil War the building was never completed. Its multimillionaire owner, it is said, died a year later a penniless and broken man.

In between our sightseeing we pottered about Silver Street watching the river traffic and exploring the taverns and restaurants that now burgeoned once again, their décor and their names - like Natchez Landing and Cock-of-the-Walk - evoking echoes of old Natchez-under-the-Hill. Our own Silver Street Inn was a former bordello, now adapted to comfortable tourist accommodation above a highly respectable dress shop.

The *Mississippi Queen*, modern sister ship of the *Delta Queen*, called in while we were there looking rather like a floating Holiday Inn with a sternwheel stuck on the back. Highly unexpected was our first and only encounter with long distance canoeists. We rushed down to the wharf to greet them as they pulled in - a couple of lean young men who had left Lake Itasca only a few weeks earlier. We consoled ourselves with the thought they were half our ages and in a hurry. In fact, earlier that year the canoeing record for the Mississippi had been broken by the remarkable partnership of 61-year-old Verlen Kruger and 33-year-old Valerie Fons, who paddled the entire length, night and day, in 23 days, 10 hours and 20 minutes. We were in correspondence with them later as they were about to embark on a 20,000-mile plus paddle embracing North and South America.

We also spent half a day across the river in Vidallia. Here in the surrounding flat lands lay most of the plantations that once belonged to the fine families of Natchez. A lot of them were being turned over to soya bean and milo, but at least we saw our first cotton blooming and fingered the fluffy tufts whose final destination might be anywhere in the world. Back in Memphis a cotton broker had told us that today's machinery could gather in the harvest fifty times faster than the average human picker. It must have been a devastating innovation for the mainly Black work force, and the effects of it were everywhere to be seen in the abandoned shanties of the Mississippi landscape.

On our last night we dined on catfish at the Cock-of-the-Walk. While we watched the sun go down in a spectacular blaze behind the bridge we discussed a proposition that George had been mulling over for some time. Everyone had forewarned us that the 130-mile stretch of river from Baton Rouge to New Orleans was both extensively canalised and industrialised. It also carried a heavy traffic of ocean-going vessels. We were relatively unperturbed by the prospect of these for we had already experienced ocean-going vessels on the lower reaches of the Danube and found their wash rather less troublesome than that of many far smaller craft. But from all accounts it would be an exceedingly tedious plod, hemmed in by high levees with oil refineries and barge terminals providing the principal scenic features.

Prodding at a tourist map of Louisiana George now suggested we left the main river just below Baton Rouge and followed one of the old distributaries down to the Gulf.

"There won't be much current," he warned, "but we'll be travelling through the heart of real delta country." But as far as I was concerned the idea hardly needed selling as I gazed happily at the innocuous-looking blue thread representing Bayou Lafourche.

We rang Baton Rouge to consult Faye Russell at the Louisiana Office of Tourism. She thought it was a great idea and I even detected a note of relief in her voice. "I'll fix for someone to meet y'all at the ferry landing at St Francisville," she said. "The final approach to Baton Rouge is kinda dismal."

Right from the earliest planning stages of our journey Faye had been the one person who consistently supported and encouraged the enterprise. Her faith in the eccentric plans of two strangers had been quite touching, as was the concern she had since manifested for our welfare. In fact I had started telephoning her intermittently to report our progress from as far back as Hannibal, Missouri, at which point she had said encouragingly but guardedly "It's great y'all are doing fine. Mind, there's a little ways to go yet. But keep in touch." We already seemed to have travelled so far by then that I had overlooked the 1000-plus miles still remaining.

Now there were just 100 miles to go to St Francisville. It would be our longest stretch without any pre-arranged landfall and we knew we must allow a minimum of four days - and be prepared for more. When we set off it was with the heaviest load yet, our food box packed to the brim with cans and packets, every available container filled with water, and our cooler crammed with ice.

Since Vicksburg the sense of doom that had bedevilled so many of my days had been lulled by a period of fine weather, delightful camp sites and the reviving interludes of good company and pampered living. But the thought of 100 unbroken miles of exposure to the whims of the river was not a happy one and I was full of foreboding that our run of luck was due for a hiccup. In the event it was justified. Or maybe forebodings bring their own negative deserts.

We got off to a slow start: stifling heat unalleviated by even a whisper of breeze, and a miserable current. Much of the first 10 miles was taken up by one of the Mississippi's more extravagant contortions with a sand bar pushing us to its extremes. There was a whole series of sand bars for much of the day, one of them offering a lunch site that would have been exceedingly pleasant if it had not been for the mind-saturating heat.

How we could have done with those sand bars later on. Quite suddenly they petered out. On either side of the river banks alternated between revetment and low cliffs of soft soil beneath an overhang of shrubbery. Then in the distance the sky growled.

It had been some time since we experienced a storm while actually on the river and the miserable fear I'd come to associate with them had receded to the edges of consciousness. Now it took only that distant grumble to bring incipient panic scuttling to the forefront. Soon the grumbling was no longer distant.

"We ought to get off the river," I said as casually as I could. George grunted. We had canoed 29 miles and were tired anyway. But the alternating revetment and low cliffs seemed to have no end. The charts gave no encouragement either; rather the contrary. With some restraint I refrained from comment as I saw we had just launched into a 10-mile reach called Dead Mans Bend.

The sky deepened to blue-black and there was no longer any hope that we might escape the full brunt of the storm. A landing could be delayed no longer. As soon as we stepped out of the canoe we sank up to our knees in mud but, with energy born of great urgency, managed to extricate ourselves, haul the We-no-nah out of the water, unload the camping gear, upturn the canoe and pitch the tent on the least soft and least steep patch of ground we could find in time that was fast running out. The rain started as we shoved in the final pegs.

Initially there were two alleviating factors. Firstly there was little wind or undoubtedly the tent would have collapsed rather soon. Secondly it was early evening and still daylight of sorts, albeit turned into sepulchral gloom by a sky weighed down with sinister intent. Otherwise the following hours were of unmitigated awfulness. I gave up all pretence of bravery, filled with a terrible premonition that this time the river had determined to get us. There was literally nowhere to escape to from this wretched strip of mud caught between the river and crumbling cliff, and the noise of the deluge on the tent, the exploding sky overhead and searing, almost continuous lightning possessed my mind completely.

Then the ground sheet began to sink as water started to flow under the tent itself. As George scrambled out into the holocaust I yelled at him to come back, then in a desperate bid to hold on to reason tried babbling out the words of a prayer that had rescued me many times in life's more trying circumstances. "God grant me the serenity to accept the things I cannot change..." An urgent scraping sound began to penetrate my fear. "...Courage to change the things I can..." Beneath me the ground sheet stopped sinking. "...And the wisdom to know the difference." The scraping sound continued.

I stopped snivelling and crawled out into the sodden uproar. "What are you doing?" George couldn't hear, but I could see. Using one of our cooking pans he had dug a trench curving round above and down either side of the tent. Already twin torrents scurried along it down to the river carrying the water away from our tiny refuge. "Courage to change the things I can," I thought and felt very ashamed.

But fear still had the upper hand as George shouted something from which I caught "...check...canoe". I yelled after him but was incapable of following. Crouching in the tent entrance I watched wretchedly as the lightning revealed his floundering progress through the mud. I saw him haul the canoe further up on the shore, wedge the painter under stones, secure items we had abandoned in our haste. Behind him and veiled by the hurtling rain the river was like molten lead. Fork lightning ripped along it in jagged, lunatic procession in fearsome concert with the detonating sky.

It was terrible but also, finally, hypnotic and very beautiful, and by the time George returned I was standing outside the tent quite uselessly but with some kind of absurd logic in the justice of us both being exposed to whatever might befall. The worst of the storm lasted a couple of hours then it moved ever so slowly away, and by 10 p.m. all was benign and still under a clear starlit sky. We pottered about ineffectually trying to mop up and getting a meal together by lamplight. A tow passed with a million mayflies cavorting in its searchlight and, as it flickered briefly over us, several thousands of them transferred to our lamp. We retreated into the tent and left them to it and next morning had to scrape off layers of their fishy corpses before we could decamp.

At least after such a storm the night was relatively cool. As we lay in the tent listening to the throb of another passing tow I said "You were marvellous. Thanks. I can't seem to cope with this bloody river any more. Not that there's much choice is there? And tomorrow we've got this Atchafalya thing to face."

"It'll be all right, you'll see," George said, which was

so predictable that at least it made me smile.

We'd had our first hint of potential problems with the Atchafalya way back in St Louis when we met Claude Strauser, a technician with the Corps of Engineers. Producing texts, charts and graphs, Claude had launched into a long and technical discourse on the vast resources of funds, time, energy and expertise dedicated to devising and executing methods of controlling the river. Having by then long established my own uneasy relationship with the Big Muddy I viewed with some scepticism the idea of anyone at all controlling her. And then I warmed to Claude completely as, with a wry grin and a dismissive wave of an arm at his pile of papers, he concluded:

"But I guess what it really comes down to is learning to listen to what the river is telling us, and then trying to do what she says. We did a lot of wrong things in the past. The cut-offs we made, for instance - she didn't like 'em, not at all. So she tore down her banks, scoured out different channels, threw up new sand banks, and scattered our fine plans every which-way. We keep trying though and I guess some of the time we get it right. And when it comes to the Atchafalya, we've just gotta get it right. Ask them about the Atchafalya when you get to Vicksburg."

So we did. Vicksburg is the headquarters of the Corps of Engineers on the Lower Mississippi. Here they operate their Waterways Experimental Station which began long ago as a small hydraulics laboratory and now covers 700 acres with some of the most sophisticated equipment of its kind in the world. Herbert Kassner had shown us round huge sheds where sections of the Mississippi and other water systems were re-created to scale so that they could be subjected to simulated forces of nature in any of a variety of combinations, and the results fed into computers. Vital studies had been done here in preparation for the D-Day landings in World War II we were told; but it was our river that interested us more just then.

"Yeah," Herbert Kassner said when we enquired about the Atchafalya, "that's bin some headache," and led us straight to the model which showed why.

During her restless history the river's relationship with her various tributaries and distributaries had changed often and dramatically, but never more dramatically than her developing involvement with the Atchafalya over a period of nearly 200 years. Even with a small scale map you did not need to be an engineer to conclude that the Big Muddy's shortest and most natural route to the Gulf of Mexico was by means of the Atchafalya. Left to her own devices there would be no stopping her.

"Which would be kinda inconvenient for Baton Rouge and New Orleans," Herbert Kassner observed as we surveyed the model showing how these two great ports would be left high and dry. "Not to speak of the industrial plants and tens of thousands of acres of plantations that would lose their fresh water resources, and the tens of thousands more that would be engulfed. So there's no way we can let it happen."

They thought they'd solved the problem in 1963 when a series of expensive structures were completed to control the flow of water from the Mississippi by means of an Outflow Channel into the Atchafalya. Ten years later phenomenal floods had put it all at great risk and another multi-million dollar system of structures and channels inaugurated.

"Hopefully we can soon all breathe easy," Herbert Kassner said, adding thoughtfully, "though there's some that say we'll never stop her having her way."

"We're told the currents are pretty tricky where the systems meet," I said.

"In high water they can be real bad - especially when the Control Structure's operational. Unpowered or disabled vessels risk getting sucked in. But there's warning signs and a rescue vessel on permanent stand-by. And the water's dropped a lot. Keep well over on the left bank and you'll be OK".

But I hadn't liked the sound of it one little bit.

The junction with the Outflow Channel lay a mere 20 miles downstream from our stormbound camp site. With my confidence battered by the previous evening's experience I viewed the prospect without joy. After a coolish night the great heat and humidity had returned. Our water supplies were adequate but we had exhausted the ice and there were still three days to go. The thought of St Francisville, 90 miles ahead, seemed like a pearl beyond price, and just about as unattainable.

"Remember we *must* stay over by the left bank," I kept saying to George, miles before we got there.

Well ahead we saw the warning notice. On our charts the message was spelt out in red "very dangerous currents.... A flashing amber light ....indicates structures operational ...vessels should navigate as close to the left descending bank ...as safety will permit."

But in the end, to my indescribable relief, it was all a bit of a damp squib. There were no flashing amber lights and though the current was brisk the water had dropped to such a level that there was little fear of losing control. Across the river we could see the Corps of Engineers' rescue vessel moored just beyond the entrance to the Outflow Channel.

"How about seeing if they've any ice to spare?" George suggested, and it seemed a fine idea.

The crew, surprised and delighted to have the tedium interrupted by unexpected visitors, did better than that. They refilled our water containers, plied us with coffee, served us up a hot meal, and sent us off with a box of cookies. They also confirmed the presence of extensive sand bars a few miles downstream. One of these proved an ideal camp site and the presence of a small holiday resort on the opposite shore, with jonboats pottering about the river, gave the comforting feeling we had once more rejoined the human race.

Forty-five miles and, with luck, rather less than two days to go. As far as we knew there were no further hazards but I was far too twitchy to take this for granted. The main feature of the next day was Angola Landing and its ferry crossing serving the Louisiana State Penitentiary. A huge sand bar formed an island in the middle of the river at this point, the navigation channel skirting it along the right bank. The left bank channel looked unobstructed and fast and would save us probably a mile, so we headed for that. The prison buildings lay invisible behind acres of bottomlands swamp and forest and a double line of levees. All the same an official boat roared across to take a closer look at us, but went away again presumably satisfied we were not about to make rendez-vous with some fugitive from justice.

Our chosen channel was very fast indeed and we fair zipped along. We learned later that several prisoners had perished while attempting to swim across it to freedom. As we came out of the particularly long bend of fast water we hit a fierce back eddy at the same time as the re-bounding wash from a passing upstream tow. The turbulence surging from the rear and the current carrying us backwards into it created an extremely uncomfortable impasse from which we eventually could only extricate ourselves by back-paddling into the worst of the churning waters until the current finally picked us up and bounced us through and out of it.

We had made good progress with every hope of breaking our daily paddling record, but it was not to be. Around mid-afternoon the sky darkened ominously. One look at the charts warned that we were back in a prolonged section of revetment interrupted at only one point by a peninsula that might be camp-worthy. It turned out to be too exposed to be ideal but a thousand times better than our strip of mud two days earlier. And this time the gods were with us. For an hour or two huge bastions of black cloud surged overhead but on this occasion their evil load was destined to fall elsewhere.

In the early afternoon next day we entered the long last straight stretch to the landing at St Francisville and saw, miles ahead, the ferry itself chugging back and forth across the river. It was as hot and as airless as it had ever been and the current negligible near the left bank from which I adamantly refused to distance myself. I kept repeating silently that we were nearly there, that nothing, but nothing could possibly go wrong. But the proximity of St Francisville seemed contained in an unreality quite unrelated to the steaming heat and tired muscles and creeping progress of the here-and-now. George was suffering badly from dehydration and we rode the water briefly while we organised a drink from our tepid water supply.

Then at last we were there. In the hurry to get behind the protection of the landing stage and haul the canoe up on the muddy shore before the ferry returned, there was no time to savour the moment. As we straightened up from our efforts the ferry eased in and a voice, god-like, came from the sky. "Are y'all the British guys we've bin waitin' for? We bid y'all welcome."

We looked at each other and grinned in exquisite realisation. We'd made it. Well, almost.

Chapter Eleven
"Where y'all going?"

"Sheer heaven," concluded my notes written at the end of the day we reached St Francisville. David Floyd had come to pick us up by truck. We'd stopped for iced drinks at a store and then swilled gallons more in the cosy living room of his home in the grounds of antebellum Oakley House.

David was in charge of restoration work on this fine plantation home whose 100-acre grounds were a showpiece of Louisiana's exuberant vegetation. It was here that the great bird artist Audubon had done some of his earliest work while employed as a tutor in the 1820s. Apparently he had roamed these lovely woodlands shooting a prodigious number of birds to get enough specimens from which to perfect his famous works. In the end the family had sent him away; perhaps they became weary of so many corpses.

Somewhere along the route from Natchez we had paddled out of the cotton lands of the Mississippi's alluvial plains into the vast historic sugar bowl of Louisiana. There was little sign of it though as we drove into Baton Rouge next morning past vast petro-chemical works. Only a few decades ago the 40-ft channel dredged in the Mississippi had opened up the final 240 miles from the Gulf to Baton Rouge for ocean-going freighters and tankers. In its wake followed the maze of pipe lines and industrial installations. "So Louisiana sold her soul for cash," David commented drily. "The plantations died and the countryside disappeared. Well a lot of it anyway." We'd heard Baton Rouge described as the gateway to the petro-chemical Ruhr of America. More than ever Bayou Lafourche seemed a good idea.

It was grand to meet Faye Russell in Baton Rouge and find a gentle lady matching the gentle voice that had imparted so much telephonic encouragement in past weeks. In no time all was arranged. One of David's assistants would drive us downstream to Donaldsonville and pop us in at Bayou Lafourche.

Faye gave us a list of contacts along the route. "Y'all are going to have a great time," she said. "The people along those bayous are something real special; for us too it's another world down there in Cajun country. You know about the Cajuns I guess?" We did, a bit. They were the descendants of French-speaking Acadians who had drifted here after deportation by the British from Nova Scotia in the 1750s in one of the less pretty episodes of our history.

There was only time to get a brief impression of the fragments of the old Baton Rouge that survived beneath the industrial overlays. We spent most of it in the Rural Life Museum learning about the unenviable lot of Black plantation workers in the 19th century.

On our last evening the weather maps on our hotel TV were accompanied by disquieting talk of tropical disturbances gathering momentum out in the Gulf. The weather presenter got quite excited about it offering a series of hypotheses as to when and where it might burgeon into a legitimate hurricane and hit the coast. One of his top choices appeared to be more or less at the far end of Bayou Lafourche. But over breakfast next morning Faye was reassuring. Tropical disturbances, it seemed, came and went in the Gulf like April showers in the Home Counties. "If we get a bad one there's plenty of warning and everyone knows what to do," she said. I hoped they'd remember to tell us too.

Bayou Lafourche is known as the world's longest street. Frequently subject to flood the bayou had long been blocked off from its Mississippi parent by a spillway. From time to time this was opened to let water through, but it looked pretty murky when we launched on to it from a patch of meadow just round the corner from a garage and supermarket.

After the Big Muddy it was rather like embarking on an over-sized ditch, and before many yards we were paddling between twin borders of trees and tangled shrubs. It was really quite pretty if you didn't look too closely, when you noticed that it also acted as a garbage dump for some of the local inhabitants. Fairly soon we saw the metallic blue flash and white belly of our first Louisiana heron and slid beneath a gang of squabbling catbirds; but otherwise the immediate quiet was almost uncanny. We had not realised how much our ears had grown accustomed to the changing but constant sounds of the Mississippi. Now, instead, we were rarely free of the alien hum of traffic, invisible beyond the screen of vegetation. The air was quite still; so was the water. We stopped paddling for a while to watch a piece of flotsam creep alongside the bank.

"Half a mile per hour?" I hazarded. "If we let her drift we might make the Gulf in 15 days."

"You're forgetting the tide as we get further down," George said helpfully. "On a flood-tide we'll be going backwards."

In the coming days we reckoned we were doing very well if we averaged three miles an hour. But that first day we had launched late and we did not plan to travel far.

Thus we discovered the first basic problem as the "world's longest main street" proved to be just that. In the long ago days before the roads came it had made sense for the early settlers to build their homesteads right on the bayou banks, clearing and cultivating wide wedges of land that extended as far back as the nearest swamp. As the land was sub-divided through successive generations the strips of cultivation became more and more narrow, the houses more and more numerous. Now they formed an almost continuous chain in what must surely be the world's longest and narrowest example of urban development. As far as camp sites were concerned it rated zero.

Soon we caught glimpses of the first houses. Their occupants fell into two categories: the majority who left the bayou banks to their own wilderness devices and those who hacked away painstakingly to create gardens with smooth green lawns reaching right to the water's edge. Either way we had a problem.

"Looks as though we're going to have to camp in someone's backyard," George observed as the hot sultry afternoon wore on into an only marginally less hot sultry evening.

We selected an immaculate lawn sloping down from a neat bungalow and, praying that we would not be observed, slunk across the garden to the front door.

"We're sorry to bother you," I said to the questioning middle-aged face that peered round the door, "but is there anywhere along the bayou where we might camp?" He looked bemused but not antagonistic so I added "We're British canoeists: the canoe is moored just there, at the bottom of your lawn."

"Well I'll be darned," he said at last and, turning back, called "Hi Mom. Two Britishers ...canoeists ...wanna camp."

Half an hour later our tent was pitched on the first grass it had felt for many weeks, and not long after our host and hostess came down with cans of beer and a local reporter who interviewed us by torchlight amidst the gathering mosquitoes.

The gambit had worked so well that we repeated it for the remainder of our progress down the bayou and it never failed. One young lady, living in a caravan above a shore line fringed with cypress trees, actually thanked us for "choosing my yard". Then there was the Swanner family. Their young son was mowing the lawn when we approached him. He disappeared with alarmed alacrity, subsequently explained by his mother Rebecca who told us there had been a spate of kidnaps in the area and the poor lad had been convinced his turn had come. He soon recovered and helped us pitch our tent after Rebecca announced, "Sure you can camp. I've just this minute put the paper down from reading about y'all. Of course y'all will dine with us."

Her husband was in oil like most of the men in the neighbourhood, Rebecca told us, usually working seven days on, seven days off which a lot of them spent shrimping. Sure it could be lonely for the women but as a former nurse she was something of a magnet for lame ducks, some of them literally so. The mallards whose peace we had disturbed with our arrival were among those she had nursed back to health and had expressed their gratitude by setting up permanent home on the premises. There had been a dramatic sequel earlier in the year when they produced their first brood.

"The babes started disappearing one by one, and one day I saw why. There was this alligator caught in the act, grabbing one of *my* little ducks out of *my* garden and slinking back into the bayou. It was real terrible. So I called the Wild Life and Fish Refuge, and guess what they said? No, I could no way shoot a protected animal outa season. Who's gonna protect my ducks I demanded? So in the end they sent a guy round to set some bait and shoot the old devil."

With days much shorter now and the mosquitoes as active as ever there was little choice once dusk had fallen than to retire into the tent and there quietly swelter. Thus when in due course we crept into Thibodaux "where yesterday welcomes tomorrow" to be met by Lee Martin of the Chamber of Commerce we accepted joyously the offer of a couple of nights air-conditioned b. and b.

Sandy, one of the Holiday Inn's receptionists, took us for a drive through the countryside. Out on the sugar plantations it was the replanting season and we stopped to watch stems of mature cane being laid out along furrows and covered with soil. In due course new plants would spring from the nodules in the old cane.

"It'll be three years before it can be harvested," Sandy said. "So it ties up a lotta land and capital."

It explained why sugar cane needed to be grown on a large scale and why the industry had come late to Lafourche. The Cajuns preferred their smaller holdings of cotton, corn, rice and peas, or harvesting the fruits of the sea. It had taken the know-how and investment of sugar planters from other areas to establish the industry here.

Sugar apart, Sandy told us, small farms were still the norm and a form of share-cropping quite widely practised.

"The land's bin divided up so often over the years," She explained.

"And a lotta folks don't wanna farm any more anyway. Our family, for instance - we've gotten 38 acres and lease it out to the same family as my parents and their parents did before them, and so it goes from one generation to the next. We get a percentage of the crop value. Some share croppers will lease from several landowners like us so they gotten enough acreage to make a living." It was Sandy who explained, too, that owning or leasing land was one thing; what lay beneath it was quite another. Land could be sold but the mineral rights retained for several years entitling the owner to a percentage of any successful exploitation. As the oil boom unfolded many had lived to regret the disposing of such rights on seemingly useless marsh in order to earn the proverbial quick buck.

Back in Thibodaux we set off with Lee to do the city sights. These included the cemetery which did turn out to have its peculiar fascination. Because of the delta's high water table, normal graves were liable to disgorge their coffins in a way that must have been very upsetting. The problem had been resolved by building family mausoleums above ground, some of immense proportions and elaborate embellishment, their inscriptions witness to the generations finally put to rest within them. I counted 38 names on one monument dating back to the mid-19th century. Newer space-saving tiered structures looked like luggage lockers at a railway station, some already occupied, others empty but many inscribed with the names of their future occupants. "Sure I already booked mine," Lee said as though it was as natural as arranging next year's holiday. Which, after all, it was.

Before heading on down the bayou we took up an invitation to spend a couple of days at Houma, some distance to the south on another bayou. One of the main purposes was to meet Annie Miller, now in her seventies, who had built up an unparalleled knowledge of the flora and fauna of the delta. But it was her rapport with alligators that had made her a legend far beyond the frontiers of Louisiana.

Intrigued we set out by motor boat with her one late afternoon to penetrate the labyrinthine waters of the delta. Here in this huge soggy wilderness where the Mississippi's multitudinous waters finally seep out into the open sea the unwary could be lost forever in a maze of minor waterways through land that barely qualified as such and certainly offered no landfall. Some of the minor bayous were so choked with vegetation that it would not have been possible to travel far along them anyway. Predominant were the water hyacinths, very pretty with their delicate mauve flowers. We had noticed patches of them earlier here and there as we paddled down Lafourche.

Annie snorted when we pointed them out. "That," she said "is what comes of messin' with Mother Nature. Some Japanese guy brought them in, mebbe 100 years ago, at a big cotton exhibition in New Orleans. He gave one to every visitor to his booth and everyone thought they were real pretty like you said. What he didn't say was that the darned things are self-pollinating and double their numbers every two weeks! So when everyone found their fish ponds and pools gettin' choked up they threw the stuff into the bayous, and then there was no holdin' it. Everything's been tried - forking, special machinery, arsenic, even flame throwers."

Soon we reached and briefly travelled along the wide waters of the Intracoastal Waterway, the huge channel linking northern Florida with Texas. On one side of its broad ribbon stretched swamp in infinite acres, on the other floating marsh. The first, Annie explained, was wet but anchored; the second literally floated. She turned off into a minor bayou threading through a section of cypress swamp. The venerable cypress trees, festooned in veils of Spanish moss, actually stood in water from which protruded the Disneyesque nodules or "knees" through which their submerged roots acquired necessary sustenance from the air.

Finally Annie brought the boat to a halt and cut the engine. Never empty, never quiet, the delta wilderness impinged itself on our senses in a chorus of squeaks and warbles and snufflings and lonely haunting cries. As the light drained from the sky and dusk crept and thickened across marsh and swamp we watched the movements of great white egrets, a glorious straggling formation of white ibis, a pair of great blue herons, and a family of nutria playing on the banks. But Annie was hugely disappointed.

"Normally there's far, far more. Why, only two days ago there were egrets, herons, spoonbills like you wouldn't believe - the sky just full of 'em. And ducks everywhere." The reason for such paucity was in no doubt in Annie's mind. The alligator season, which lasted only 30 days, had begun just two days earlier. This was an easily accessible and rewarding area for the hunter; no wonder, Annie said grimly, most wildlife had fled.

Gently we chugged across to some bushes overhanging the bayou so "y'all can see what those killers get up to." Shooting alligators in the water was profitless to the hunter for the creature would simply sink and spoil. The accepted method was to suspend bait of raw chicken from overhanging branches. Thus hooked the alligator was a sitting target when the hunter next came to check his bait. In order to protect the young no alligator of less than 4 ft. in length could be shot and thus there was a minimum height at which the bait should be set. Many a hunter, however, blatantly bent the rules.

"Y'all look at that," Annie said, incensed, as we approached some bait only inches above the water. Angrily she yanked it up higher with a boat hook. I suspected she must have been the alligator hunters' least favourite person.

But if the hunting season had frightened off other wild life, it did not seem to have made much impact on the alligators themselves. Having satisfied herself that all visible bait conformed to the regulations Annie set about her daily routine of meeting her strange friends. In her attempt to thwart the hunters she had brought even larger quantities than usual of their favourite fare on the principle that if they had their fill they would be less tempted by the hunter's bait. So, with our engines still, we rode the water as Annie leaned over the stern and called in ringing tones "Baby ...Baby Dee ...Bay-bee ..Come on Baby ... Charlie ...Chaar-lee ...Come on now ...Arthur ...Is that you Arthur? ...Bay-bee - where are you?"

For a few moments nothing happened and then, one by one

and from every direction, snouts broke the surface of the water and headed towards us. Soon we were encircled by alligators of all ages and sizes, glinting eyes fixed on the large lumps of raw chicken that Annie proffered at the end of a stick, jaws ready to snap, briefly revealing rows of razor teeth that emphasised her warnings to us not to lean our arms on the gunwales. I can't say I shared this tough, gentle lady's quite patent devotion to her unbeautiful protegées; but it was an experience to remember.

After Annie's swamp tour the banks of Bayou Lafourche seemed like the height of civilisation. As we left Thibodaux behind us the heat and humidity were as unrelenting as ever. The fish had never been so active, mullett especially leaping out of the water a foot at a time, flanking our progress like so many outriders, but at times so close they only just missed landing in the canoe. On several occasions we saw nutria, frequently snakes and once a squirrel swimming hard across the bayou, its bushy tail trailing in the water behind it.

And the bayou itself was changing. Gradually it widened, became a little less enclosed, the banks lower, the thick vegetation replaced by areas of the tall grasses and reeds characteristic of the marshes. It also became busier. Fairly soon we passed our first shipyard and from then on boat building, commercial wharfs, jack-up barges, crew boats for the oil rigs, pleasure launches, skiffs became increasing features of the passing scene.

We had our first contact with the bayou's shrimping fleet which developed into a colourful collection of all sizes from skiffs that went out for the day to medium and large vessels with trawls or "butterflies" that might be out from a few days to three weeks. The "butterflies" were distinctive structures like butterfly wings that lowered the nets both port and starboard while the vessel rode the water and let the current bring in the catch. A lot of shrimpers complained of a bad season, blaming it variously on freshwater intrusion, oil rig snags and spillage and "them big guys out in the Gulf grabbin' the goddarn females 'fore they can lay their eggs." And we met our first pirogue, traditional flat-bottomed craft of the bayou, though now mostly kept for probing swamp and marsh where the most sophisticated modern vessel would have been useless.

Even though the bayou was now wider there was little manoeuvring space to get out of anyone's way and after our experiences on the Big Muddy we were gratefully surprised whenengineswerethrottledbackasmotorisedvesselsapproached us in what we assumed to be an act of common courtesy. Cajun friends laughed when we reported this. "Sure they do. It's not so far back that anyone who rocked a Cajun in his pirogue as like as not got a shot across his bows!"

It was near Houma we'd had our first close contact with the Cajuns. The Dusenbery family ran a Cajun restaurant called La Trouvaille in the simple little house in which Wilma and Gene Dusenbery reared the family of twelve children they had produced in a span of 11 years. Now mostly married themselves eight of them were there to help cook and serve plates piled high with chicken gumbo, rice and sweet peas to the coachload of Californians with whom we coincided that day. Afterwards they grouped on the porch and sang Cajun songs for us in sweet harmony, including the haunting story of Evangeline.

I had come across Evangeline, or rather her statue, some years earlier on a visit to Nova Scotia. She typified the tragedy of the French-speaking Acadians. Completely dispossessed of land and livestock by the British for refusing to bear arms against their compatriots the Acadians were deported, families split, women often separated from husbands or lovers, fathers from sons, brothers from sisters. The Evangeline of Longfellow's sad romantic poem became the symbol of their despair as she sought her lost love far and wide.

A fair proportion of the Acadians eventually found their way to this remote corner of Louisiana already largely populated by the French. It was not only remote but isolated and the soggy landscapes and hot, steamy climate of the delta must have made a bewildering contrast with the austere beauty of their former homelands. But the Acadians had learned to thrive in adversity and they adapted their farming, fishing and hunting techniques, survived and flourished. Likewise their culture evolved as "Acadian" became "Cajun" and intermarriage injected new elements which became embodied in their unique culture.

In due course this too was threatened. Compulsory attendance at public schools was accompanied by a ban on spoken French on school premises. New roads bored their way alongside the bayous bringing modernisation and the American way of life. World War II transplanted young Cajuns from their bayous to many corners of the globe from which they returned with new skills and new aspirations that were easier to fulfill in the cities than in their native swamps. Finally through television American-language culture bombarded that last Cajun stronghold, the home.

But the saga isn't finished yet. In recent years a reversal of attitudes has made Cajun French not only acceptable, but even respectably "ethnic". What was once a derisive term is now bandied proudly on T-shirts, bumper stickers, souvenirs and restaurant menus. There are Cajun-language radio and television programmes and, at last, a series of books on Conversation Cajun French. The simple dedication is to "the millions of Cajuns who preserved the Cajun French language by word of mouth despite ridicule and legal prohibition".

Like others who have survived oppression or exploitation, the Cajuns developed - and indeed cherished - a macho image. They hunt and fish prodigiously and not always discriminately and some, it seemed, were not averse to taking the law into their own hands. It had its less attractive aspects as we discovered while demolishing huge piles of fresh shrimps one day at a Cajun supper party. George happened to comment on how few Blacks we had seen in recent days and was rapidly enlightened by a fellow guest. "They know better'n come down here," he grunted, barely pausing in his task of swift dissection. "An' if they don't there's always the white silk cord..."

It was something of a relief later that day to meet another Cajun of equally passionate but more gentle disposition. Some years earlier Skip Cheramie had converted himself from an avid hunter to a dedicated and talented artist. The art of decorative duck decoys, handed down from one generation to the next, had a long tradition in the delta though Skip was largely self-taught. He told us how he would spend three months studying a duck in the wild and in pictures before he would even put a knife to a block of wood. A dead bird lost its colour very rapidly but that wasn't the main reason he didn't hunt any more, he explained, as we watched him turn a square lump of tupelo wood into the recognisable beginnings of a shoveler.

"I just got sickened by the mass slaughter. Take the nine-day teal season. Folks round here go crazy, wanna impress their business friends so they lay on shoots that bring the teal down in their hundreds. An' what for? Just to be carried off to show the folks wherever they're from how smart they've bin."

We watched in silence as the shoveler slowly began to acquire not only shape but character. "How long will it take you to make the finished article?" I asked.

"'Bout 90 hours I guess."

We understood why when Skip picked up the well-advanced head of a teal and began creating new dimensions before our eyes as he burnt in delicate feather strokes, and with a tiny knife cut minuscule detail in the upper and lower mandibles. Later every feather would be painted over and over again until the colour was perfected.

"What happens if you do go badly wrong?"

Skip grinned. "Waal, I guess you can always turn a duck into a canary."

Our progress down the final stretches of the bayou was excruciatingly slow. "You'd think," I said half way through a morning of weary crawl, "that after all this time we'd be able to do better than this."

"Not with a zero current and not in this heat," George said consolingly.

I had long given up the pleasant anticipation of cooling breezes off the approaching sea. Indeed any breeze was likely to be more than we bargained for. Hurricane Diane had hit the North Carolina coast a few days earlier. Now a new tropical disturbance had spawned in the Gulf, its progress being charted every time we switched on the radio or TV in Thibodaux. To the accompaniment of a barrage of maps and arrows and swirling isobars, the weather men made pronouncements in the same confident tones used for selling breakfast cereals and washing powders, but I suspected our guess was as good as theirs.

One of the local radio stations had even supplied us with a chart telling us "How to track a hurricane" which meant essentially staying tuned in to KTIB, Thibodaux' radio station. For days on end it had felt as though a storm must break. And finally it did.

We made it just in time to a deserted commercial wharf, hastily covered our more valuable gear and beat a hurried retreat into a large shed which had surprisingly been left open. The crashing thunder and rain drumming on the tin roof made such a hullabaloo that we did not hear Hilda come in. It was her husband's shed, she said, but seemed quite pleased to find two bedraggled foreigners sheltering in it.

When the rain eased briefly we sloshed across to the bungalow to meet Eddie, have coffee and be shown photographs of their previous home, destroyed completely in a tornado twenty years earlier.

"Didn't you think of starting up again somewhere else?" I asked, knowing that I would. But Hilda's expression showed it had not even occurred to her.

When they suggested we camped in the big shed we did not hesitate. The storm ranted much of the night but by the time we were summoned to breakfast at the bungalow next morning all was still, bright and cool.

"Only 17 miles to go," George said as we slid away from the wharf. It was hard to take it in.

With the bayou now quite exposed to the roads that pursued it closely on both sides it was a little like paddling down the central reservation of a motorway. Now small-town America unfolded alongside us in slow motion: motels, hotels, shopping malls, banks, insurance offices, pizza huts, Macdonalds, the Full Gospel Tabernacle and Paw Paw helter skelter, lawn and garden centres and gas stations, iced beer parlours and more iced beer.

And in the end, too, it was something of a royal progress for if the roads were now exposed to us, so were we exposed to them. At first we thought the cars were honking at each other but then realised these were greetings aimed at us. Arms waved, voices called. Several times we were summoned to the bayou's bank. "Where y'all from ...An' where y'all going?"

"Minnesota," we answered to the first and, at last with triumphant confidence, "The Gulf", to the second.

Then on the right bank ahead of us we spied a large lady sitting on a wall. An arm was raised in greeting, plump cheeks creased with a smile of welcome. "Guess y'all are the folks we've bin waitin' for," she called. "Hi, I'm Linda." Almost simultaneously a police car screeched to a halt and the wharf suddenly became crowded with uniformed figures issuing instructions, heaving our gear out of the canoe, finally man-hauling the We-no-nah herself from the water and on to Linda's pick-up truck. It all happened so fast the momentousness of the event was over before it could be fully savoured.

Golden Meadow, journey's end. There was little evidence of the fields of golden rod that gave the place its name and in those early days guarded the secrets of the unimaginable wealth that lay beneath them. George had baulked a bit at the idea of ending the journey here for the open sea still lay 20 miles ahead, but next day we understood the wisdom of our advisers as we drove across the bleak marshscapes to Leeville, a few miles down the bayou. Once a thriving community it had literally been blown away in a series of hurricanes. Those of its inhabitants who did not abandon the bayou altogether moved back to the security of Golden Meadow - all of 2 ft above sea level.

For the next few days we ranged the strange world of the delta's fringes that was neither entirely land nor entirely sea. All the way down the bayou people had expounded their theories on the causes and effects of the constantly changing face of the delta where land was currently disappearing at the rate of 40-50 square miles a year. Saltwater intrusion was a term that kept cropping up as the explanation for most of the growing list of economic ills.

"Change the level of salt and you start getting a lotta problems," a crawfish farmer had told us as we looked out over his 80-acre pond. "For instance, a freshwater marsh can host over a hundred species of plant; a saltwater marsh only two. Start getting too much salt in the soil and you get all kinda problems with crop yields, not to mention craw fishing, oyster farming, just about everythin'."

But why, we asked, was the salt increasing and the land disappearing so disconcertingly?

It seemed that in the course of her history, the present delta was only the latest of many that the Big Muddy had spawned and abandoned. Later we saw maps showing the cataclysmic changes that had taken place in the score of years between the 1950s and 1970s as the delta literally succumbed to the sea. Even to the untutored eye it looked as though this one's days were numbered.

"Only this time," our informant continued, "It's us, stoopid and arrogant as we are, that's hurryin' along the process."

Flood and navigation control - those very schemes that made life safer for millions of riverside dwellers in ten States, and for thousands of navigators on those self-willed waters - was slowly but surely starving the delta: of the rich silt that had helped build it in the first place, and of the replenishing supplies of fresh water to maintain the pursuits that made up the delta's economy.

Many agreed that oil was a major culprit. The first off-shore wells in the 1940s had burgeoned into thousands. The delta swarmed with oilmen, tiny communities had swollen into satellites housing the influx of newcomers and providing the support systems that maintained the flow of Louisiana's black gold. Not only Louisiana's, but a high proportion of the rest of the world's too. About 20 miles out in the Gulf was the off-shore terminal of the mammoth installations of the oil consortium LOOP's Superport handling exclusively imported oil, and eventually capable of moving an unimaginable 100,000 barrels an hour through its network of pipelines.

"So we've made deeper navigation channels," was the gloomy conclusion, "built more and more pipelines, straightened out more and more bayous, and what's happened? The saline waters from the Gulf bite deeper into the land, the plants that hold it all together die, and another few square miles sink into the sea." A lot of experts were working on the problem apparently, though it was hard to see how all the conflicting interests would ever find a basis for agreement.

On a drive from Houma to Cocodrie we had seen for ourselves how those conflicting interests had combined to affect the face of the delta. At road's end, Cocodrie itself seemed the epitome of an impermanence that it denied in a dogged frenzy of activity. From the wharfs of its marine terminal, whose restaurant offered an excellent menu of crab, oyster and shrimp, it was not the open Gulf we looked out upon but the dwindling marshes. No longer empty though. Far into the distance the oil rigs poked up like the saplings of some surrealistic forest; near at hand were the residences that made up this strange little place: summer camps on their stilts, trailers, rooms to let, boats for charter. It may have been some years since the last big hurricane but it felt every bit like a place permanently looking over its shoulder - and ready to take to its heels at the first sign of trouble.

For the time being the latest tropical disturbance was moving away. On our last day Linda drove us out to Grand Isle so that we could finally see the open sea. Everyone was talking about the events of the previous night when a light plane had run out of fuel on its way from Mexico, landed on a beach near Grand Isle and been found to be carrying drugs. Some of our friends viewed the mishap with extreme cynicism. Who ever heard of a drug runner running out of gas? More like, they suggested, it was a decoy to keep the drug squad away from a more lucrative prize.

It would have been a bleak drive to Grand Isle if the marshes and reed beds, pools and channels had not been seething with herons, white pelicans, gulls, terns, wildfowl and waders. They were also peppered with hides, reed-built structures into which the hunter could glide in his pirogue and, thus concealed, command a considerable expanse of marsh with his guns. But, thankfully, it was not quite the game bird season and, enchanted, we stopped to observe the antics of this magnificent, restless throng. From time to time we passed a small community of houses built on stilts. By law the houses had to be 8 ft above the ground in these parts.

Teetering on the brink of the Gulf, Grand Isle itself was a ramshackle if sizeable sprawl, recently separated from the beach by a new levee. It was hard to understand how any of it had survived the countless vicious onslaughts of storm, tornado and hurricane, and hard to realise that a century and more ago rich plantations thrived on soil that now was saturated with salt if it had not already been claimed by the sea. In those days, too, Grand Isle really had been an island, with no bridge and no highway to link it to the outside world. It was not surprising then to learn that its oldest building was said once to belong to a pirate, for this must have been an ideal lair for the illicit goings-on of the early 19th century when Jean Lafitte had become a legend in his own time. This colourful figure, whose great grandson now ran a local gift shop, had his finger in many pies, the largest being slave traffic for those profitable plantations.

Since then the place had been battered again and again. I wondered why people still persisted in living here. Yet today Grand Isle is listed among the top ten of America's fishing spots, with thriving tourist and fishing industries and, of course, the ubiquitous paraphernalia of oil. I did not find it attractive. Perhaps the presence of the drug-running plane, stranded and heavily guarded on the beach, was a reminder of more modern pirates whose life style might be less ruffianly, but whose trafficking in suffering and death was every bit as ugly as their forerunners.

Across the bay at Grande Terre were the brick-and-shell ruins of Fort Livingston, never completed though occupied for a time by Confederate troops. As a boat lurched us round them on that wild windy day we looked at last across the sullen grey waters of the open sea.

It was not a satisfying conclusion to our odyssey but we had one last look at the Big Muddy from her big-city shores at New Orleans. Cajun friends had driven us there and a tail-coated doorman with several porters had helped us unload the canoe and lay her at rest among the Cadillacs in the underground parking lot of the Royal Sonesta Hotel in Bourbon Street. Here in this most elegant of American hostelries in the heart of New Orleans' French Quarter we "made camp" for the 77th and last time on the Mississippi.

There was a Block Party that evening. Huge smiling carnival figures wobbled high above sauntering, joggling humanity in fairground mood. Clowns tumbled, black youngsters break-danced, a bearded weirdie ran a lucky-dip, and an effigy of Elvis Presley opened its arms to embrace the world from a wrought iron balcony while balloons and streamers cascaded about our heads. Music blasted from every other doorway - jazz, country and western, Austrian oom-pah-pah. Boutiques were draped with T-shirts flaunting slogans that left little to the imagination. Signs invited us into massage parlours and strip shows, and through dark entrances there were glimpses into smoke-filled taverns. A few hundred yards away the Big Muddy rolled by, her deserted sand bars and our weeks of uneasy partnership contained in another lifetime.

Next day Mary and John Popadic, We-no-nah's agents from Baton Rouge, arrived to collect the canoe. We extricated her from among the Cadillacs and helped secure her on to the roof of their little car. I gave her a final pat on her red stern. As we watched her receding down the narrow street and disappear round a corner, I felt for George's hand. And, yes, there was something remarkably resembling a lump in my throat.